4152409

A BOOK OF LENTEN SERMONS
AND MEDITATIONS

TAKE UP THY CROSS

By
ARNDT L. HALVORSON

Augsburg Publishing House · Minneapolis

TAKE UP THY CROSS
Copyright 1949
Augsburg Publishing House

Printed and manufactured in the United States of America by the
Augsburg Publishing House, Minneapolis 15, Minnesota

PREFACE

The cross is the distinctive symbol of the Christian faith and life. It is the rallying point for our zeal, the clue to understanding the heart of God, and the directive for Christian living.

Though Jesus was crucified on the cross for us, we ourselves can never escape it. He who accepts Jesus accepts His cross, enters into the intense struggle with sin and evil in his own soul. Paul wrote, "I am crucified with Christ." His cross becomes our cross.

Our Lord commanded, "Take up thy cross and follow me." This means that the cross shall be ever with us in our personal lives, killing and making alive. And if we heed this command, the cross of Christ can become a factor in the life of our generation, by which our fellow men are led to Christ.

During Lent, particularly, our eyes are upon that cross, our steps are directed toward it. May we never falter on our journey.

CONTENTS

THE CROSS IS LIFE
Sermons for the Sundays During Lent

COME
Midweek Meditations for Lent

The Cross Is Life

SERMONS FOR THE SUNDAYS DURING LENT

Chapter One

Life is the testing

Text: Matthew 4:1-11

"Then was Jesus led up of the spirit into the wilderness to be tempted of the devil" (v. 1).

THE natural, human interpretation of "life" is often far from the truth. How often have we not said, while lounging on a park bench in the warm sun, "This is the life!" and extravagantly thrown our arms into the air as we reveled in what we thought was our freedom. And how seldom we have said it as we toiled in the shop, the field, the classroom, or the home! The human tendency is to regard "life" as something light and airy, and the less disturbing the better.

How often have we not said, with a sigh of relief, after a particularly trying period has passed, "I'm glad that's over; now I can *live*," not realizing that we were living when the sky was black.

Consider, too, how we wish our lives away. "Ah," we say, "when this is over, this debt paid, and I have money in the bank again, I can really start to live!" We think tomorrow, or next week,

or next year will bring the great moment, and
we remain blind to the possibilities of today.

We seem to be concerned only with the time
when we may rest from our labors, the day when
we shall have enough money in the bank to re-
tire, the moment when life shall cease to demand
anything more from us, and we can drift merrily
on with no cares, no worries.

This might make a good Mohammedan heaven,
but if the cross of Jesus has any impact on our
thinking, it never will coincide with Christian
living.

The secret fear of Blackie, the brave, bluster-
ing hero in the novel *Gone with the Wind,* is
the secret fear of almost everyone. Confronted
with an admiring girl who said to him, "You are
not afraid of anything, are you?" he was forced
to reply, "I am afraid of life." We fear struggle,
and so we fear life, because within ourselves we
know life is struggle.

Consider the evidence of life itself. Does not
all that we are—our bodies, our minds, our very
souls—cry out for work, for testing, for exertion?
Given nothing to do, the human being will waste
away. One of the basic laws of learning is the law
of use and disuse. Muscles unused grow flabby.
A mind unused deteriorates. A soul which is not
exercised will become weak.

It is this which the season of Lent ought to
teach us. It ought to teach us that there comes a

time in the life of all of us when we must come to grips with ourselves. It ought to remind us that life's prizes go to those who are willing to pay the price of self-renunciation, who do not shun the period of testing, of exertion.

This encounter between Satan and Jesus was the decisive battle in God's plan of salvation. The fate of the entire human race depended on the outcome. In this sense the temptation of Jesus is the start of His ministry. It was here He demonstrated the vulnerability of evil. It was here He demonstrated the invincibility of the Word of God. It was here He chose the lashing of the whip, the crown of thorns, the rejection, the cross. From this encounter Jesus saw clearly the price of victory. Here the cross was etched into His spirit.

By His choice He proclaims to us a significant fact. Life is the testing. We live when we run the race, or when we are in the thick of the battle. Life is lived in the arena, where life's issues are fought out, not in the parlor where they are discussed. Life is lived when we are being tugged to and fro to make a decision, not when life drifts on with no conflicts, no bumps. Somebody says, "I lived a lifetime in that moment." It is literally true.

By His choice He proclaims the necessity for temptation in life. It is needed to make the issue clear; it is needed to put decision into living.

Many a Bible scholar has not yet seen the issues of life in spite of all his knowledge. This is simply because his Bible knowledge has remained untested knowledge. He may know the answers to all the questions, but correct answers have little power unless they are backed by experience.

How about us? We all know that the Bible is God's revealed Word. We know that Jesus is God's Son, who died on the cross for our sins. We know that we can find God in prayer. How do we know? We know these things because we have learned them in youth, because we have heard them so often, and have, without question, accepted them as true. But perhaps all this which we assume we know is not really knowledge at all. What happens to our knowledge when it encounters a contrary line of thought? What happens when we find ourselves in a situation where everything contrives to take our knowledge from us? What happens when, in our business or student life, our comfortable knowledge is challenged? Does it stand up?

The issues are clarified in the test. Minor questions we see as minor. We are able to evaluate life and to appraise it for its deeper issues.

"Talent," said one man, "may come in solitude, but character is formed in struggle." They were not idle words which Edison spoke when he said, "Genius is 1 percent inspiration and 99 percent perspiration." We do not see, because we do not struggle. We lack insight, because we shy away from the test. If life is dealing you a body blow, it may be simply to help you see life's issues more clearly.

The struggle with temptation usually follows this peculiar pattern. Our vision is clarified by being obscured. The reasoning power in which we had gloried so much proves to be of little avail. In fact, it turns upon us and becomes our enemy. All that the mind does under the duress of temptation is to look for a way to extricate us from the mess we are in, to rationalize our surrender to the temptation. We become muddy in our thinking. Logical thoughts vanish; there is only meaningless turmoil. An incredible weariness possesses the spirit.

Now comes the crucial moment, and the reason for the testing is to make this moment—this moment of choice—inescapable. In this moment we can do one of two things: we can give up, or we can seize the only recourse available to us. The only recourse is, of course, God. Jesus refused to argue with the devil. He did not point out to him any particular reasons. He merely said, "God's Word says . . . " And, significantly, that clarified the issue. The decisive moment is when we decide to choose Jesus Christ. That is a moment of desperation. It is a moment of pure, blind, foolish faith. But it is the moment of clarification. In that moment the issue becomes clear, not from reasoning, not from our own strength, but from Jesus Christ.

A boy faced such a crisis. He was a popular fellow in school, perhaps too popular. This popularity was forcing him to go more and more in the direction of the crowd. The farther he went, the more popular he was; but within himself he felt more and more uneasy. He reasoned that his great popularity was worth the anxiety that accompanied it. He reasoned that he was strong enough to withstand temptation in the crucial moment. But suddenly he realized he was standing on the brink of disaster and that the next step might mean spiritual darkness. In desperation he turned to Jesus again, and prayed for help. A new strength came, and clarity of outlook. He came through. In the struggle he found life!

Temptations are needed also to put decision into life. It has been said that the majority of those who become lost do not rush into hell's abyss—they drift into it. The purged spirit, the spirit made whole in temptation's cauldron, has a buoyancy, an uplift, a decisiveness which is all too rare in our day.

Life is being ruined by indecision. Broadmindedness today has rapidly become no-mindedness. We need a bit more narrow-mindedness to bring back the balance. Men are like the pathetic creatures on Mt. Carmel to whom Elijah addressed

the question, "How long stand ye wavering between two opinions?" So many manage to escape
temptation by making no commitments, no de-
cisions, and so they live ineffective, indecisive
lives. They do not act upon principle, but upon
expedience.

Temptation puts decision into life. He who
does not meet it, or he who bows before it, becomes driftwood on life's currents. But he who
fights temptation through, in the light and the
interpretation of the cross, faces the days ahead
with new decisiveness.

The indecisive man has no joy in life. Life
plagues him. He cannot grow. He remains upon
a constant plateau of expedience. He moves in-
effectively, doing nothing, and his life eventually
snuffs itself out.

Decision puts joy into life. The man who is not
living outrightly for Jesus Christ can find no
happiness or contentment in Him. Each mention
of the cross makes him miserable. He cannot
enjoy life's good or life's sins, and he has no refuge.

Now decision is much a matter of the will. We
will to accept Jesus Christ, or the Bible record,
or the forgiveness of sins. And he whose will is
bent in that direction, who says to his generation,
"I have chosen Him," has found peace and joy.
He is in harmony with what he knows is right.

This decisiveness enables him to grow. He

grows in "grace and in the knowledge of Jesus Christ." The intricacies of the mind of Christ are opened; the paradoxes of the cross are revealed. And life grows. It becomes more and more natural to be Christ-like—because through constant testing a new spirit has been burned into him.

When you fight the lure of sin in the strength of the cross you can fight it constructively; and when you have fought such sins as drink, and doubt, and lust, and cynicism, in the light of the cross *and won,* your actions thereafter become more effective. After Jesus had dealt with Satan's attempts upon Himself, He was able to handle him in the affairs of others. When we have dealt with Satan in one area of our personal lives, we can deal with him in larger fields.

Life's trails are blazed by those who in the hour of temptation have discovered Jesus to be stronger than the tempter, have surrendered to Him, and thence serve Him in single-minded allegiance.

So, then, this is life, this moment of struggle and of test. Beyond one test lies another. The struggle with self and sin never ends. Does this sound too forbidding? Do you find little cheer in the prospect of such a life?

Then remember, it is quite likely that the hour of testing confronting you holds the opportunity of finding your Savior anew. For that is the implication in the stern words of Paul, "Work out

your own salvation with fear and trembling."
Remember, also, that you are not alone in the
struggle. For Jesus, "who was in all things tempted like as we are," is with us. Remember, finally,
that God, who permits the testing, "has with the
temptation made possible a way of escape." The
way of escape is the wounds of Jesus. Flee to them,
and you will experience within yourself a demonstration of His mighty power.

Chapter Two

Life is the walking

Text: Luke 9:51-62

"He steadfastly set his face to go to Jerusalem" (v. 51).

JESUS was born to endure the cross. This, the
Bible tells us plainly, was a part of the divine plan. But He was not a puppet, dangling
from a divine string, unable to do anything other
than that which was decreed. The greatness of
Jesus lies in the fact that He *chose* the cross. It
was a deliberate act of the will. Especially after
His encounter with Satan in the wilderness was
this choice clear-cut. His face was set toward Jerusalem, though He knew that in Jerusalem the
high priest, and Pilate, and the cross awaited Him.

The cross was required to fulfill Christ's Mes-
siahship. Occasionally the disciples would catch
glimpses of this cross, in a chance word, or a
deliberate revelation. It would bewilder and
frighten them. They always thought in terms of a
throne, not a cross.

There was the time when Peter tried to reason

with Jesus, telling Him that the cross would help nobody. I suppose he reminded Him that there was so much to be done here. How many missionaries have heard that? Peter must have been stunned by Jesus' rebuttal: "Get thee behind me, Satan." Then there was the time recorded in this text, when the disciples plainly and simply lost their zest for the journey, and wanted to take things easy for a time. Capernaum was so restful. People were so good to them there. Jesus was appreciated. Jerusalem—and the cross—was actually undesirable. The fierceness of Jesus' reply penetrates every heart which is trying to find a reason to "take things easy."

A chaplain said that when the fighting was heaviest, his men wanted most of all to hear about this strange march of Jesus toward Jerusalem and the cross. It struck a responsive chord in their hearts, this story of the Savior who deliberately walked into the jaws of death. Indeed, there is nothing else like it. Abraham walked a long and tortuous road to an unknown spot on the map in the face of great odds, but at the end of his trail there was a river and green pastures. The pioneers worked their toilsome way through forests and over prairies, but at the end were security and prosperity. The martyrs of Bataan clogged along to their death, but they were coerced, prodded with whips and guns; there was no choice involved.

Jesus walked toward Jerusalem, deliberately, choosing the cross. This walk to the cross is a tremendous challenge for us who are following Christ. For one thing, it tells us that there is a cross somewhere for us too, a cross which marks, not our doom, but our destiny. It tells us that the Christian must walk along a strange, lonely path into a far country. And it also tells us that the Christian, by faith, must have a vision of things not yet realized, an insight into truths not yet perceived. The Christian has a vision of the deep love of God, a vision of peace, a vision of home.

The disciples walked the way with Him, as we do. Also, like us, they often lacked the full vision of their destination, and when they did, the walk was a tiring ordeal. That was what had happened here. They were going to Jerusalem, they knew, but to them it was only a city, a religious citadel. They were amazed at their Lord's intense insistence to get there. For their part, the walk became a bother, and, in fact, distasteful. Obstacles were magnified.

It is always so when we walk without having the full vision of what awaits us at our final destination. Obstacles become stopping places, and the pathway may be lost.

This text tells us many things about the Christian life, which the early Christians, with deep insight, called a "way." The Christian has a forward look, a desire to arrive, a sense of urgency.

The Christian who has caught a glimpse of his goal and feverishly pursues it is fearful lest anything come to hinder him on his way. The Christian is like a musician working on a composition, into whose head have come the faint stirrings of a great melody, and who anxiously scribbles the notes before he loses them. The Christian is like one who is walking up steep mountain trails, and through deep forests and over broad plains, not for the pleasure of the walk, but for the glory of the destination.

When we forget this forward aspect of the Christian life, we are the losers. We talk sometimes as if we regard the Christian life as synonymous with heaven

The Christian life is not the celestial city. The Christian life is the march. We commend our scientists for their discoveries, but science is not the discovery. It is the quest. We sing so often of the Christian life as a "rest upon the way," and like to entertain the thought that it is the time we rest in the wooded glen or upon the high plateau. But the Christian life is the march itself, the struggle to arrive. It is the march to Jerusalem—and the cross.

There are obstacles on the road, as our text tells us. One of them is the obstacle of comfort. We are smothered in comfort until we have the taste for struggle removed. We see no need for struggle. We say, "We have it so good here. Why should we go on?" The Samaritans wished to detain Jesus. Certainly it looked inviting: all of life's comforts—plenty to eat, attention paid to His every wish. What an alluring picture! But we can hear Him, as He was faced with the temptation, saying, "We must leave this place. I go to Jerusalem." The disciples would have liked to remain, no doubt. It is difficult at times to see the value of struggle. It seems so fruitless. When the "Way" means dogged persistence, constant vigilance, persistent expenditure of energy, that way does not look inviting. But how many lives have lost the real significance of the Gospel message, simply because they have had no taste for the struggle it implies.

The Kingdom Road does mean struggle—struggle with life's comforts and its delusions, struggle with ourselves and our weaknesses, struggle with our supreme adversary. Jesus struggled in Gethsemane until He sweat blood. Peter struggled with himself, going down and rising up, being counted out, and yet returning for more, until by the spirit of God he became Cephas.

If we have once caught sight of the Jerusalem road we must walk it. We admire the stuff of our forefathers because they had a taste for struggle. And indeed struggle plays a part in any healthy life. A seed struggles to break through the ground which presses around it. A thinker struggles with a thought. But men become truly great when they struggle spiritually. Augustine wrestled with himself for years, plagued by his sins. He wrestled in torment and agony, but out of the struggle was born the author of the tremendous work *The City of God.*

The sadness of one addicted to drink, or gambling, or the sexual impulse, is not only that he is a victim of a degrading way of living, but still worse, that he has ceased to fight against the degradation. While there is struggle, there is life. God can resurrect one who is dead in sin, but why wait until rigor mortis has set in? Give God the life there is; He can use it, and He will enter into the struggle, and will work mightily within us, even as we fight.

How we deprive our generation of our best, as we settle back and rest content with what we are. One of the curses of the Kingdom is the man who says complacently, "I am good enough." Goodness may be there, but that goodness is *never* good enough!

He is the one who has had a vision of the grace of God and yet remains where he is, smugly satisfied with himself. He is the church member who is content with being preached at — who never prays, never reads, never worries about himself, never struggles, never fights it out.

A minister one time preached a sermon—a sermon full of witticisms, easy to listen to. At its conclusion, one of his listeners, a man with calloused hands and a burning spirit, said, "It was good, but I missed something. I did not feel he had ever struggled." Spiritual rebirth is cradled in a sweat of the soul.

We may have many high and fine enjoyments in the Christian life as we now live it, but before us all is Jerusalem, before us all is that road. I tell you bluntly: It is walked in struggle. Walk it.

Another obstacle to our progress on the road is the backward look—the constant temptation to be satisfied with the old ways, to go back where it was comfortable. If we look backward, we cannot look ahead. We lose the vision. And the prophet is right when he reminds us, "Where there is no vision, the people perish."

Think for a moment. What built this church? What built our church colleges? What impelled Paul to be a vagabond for the Gospel? What sent forth the first missionaries? Was it a sense of duty, a spirit of consecration? Yes, but it was something more, something without which the Kingdom road is not worth walking. It was a vision. They saw the Celestial City and kept it before their eyes.

The devil's most effective work is done when he limits our interest to ourselves, to a constant round of me-myself-and-mine, so that we see only the present. He is victor when he drives the vision from our eyes.

The Jerusalem road leads to the cross, and on

that cross was One who died that I might live and grow and find life. We must walk with the vision of that cross before us, as we pray in the hymn: "Hold Thou Thy cross before my closing eyes, shine through the gloom, and point me to the skies."

But the old ways are very real, are they not? The old Adam is still very powerful. He hounds our steps. "Go back, back to the days of comfortable sinning, back to the days of a dulled conscience, of sin unforgiven." At times his logic is most convincing.

Before us, however, lies our destiny, and we must not go back. Coleridge, in *The Rime of the Ancient Mariner*, writes:

"I am like one, that on a lonesome road
    Doth walk in fear and dread,
    And having once turned round walks on,
    And turns no more his head;
    Because he knows, a frightful fiend
    Doth close behind him tread."

On the Jerusalem road we are trapped. Before us lies newness of life. Back of us are the old ways. We cannot go back, we are timid about going ahead. The thought of the old becomes a spur, driving us to respond to the vision of the new.

We must have the vision if we are not to look back. We must have the vision if we are to continue on the road.

Has the Jerusalem road become meaningless, a dull, wearying routine of religious observances? Are you wondering if it is worth it? Then catch the vision Jesus gives us, of a new life, and run after it. Casting all else aside, stretch forth in the spirit of Paul toward the "mark for the prize of the high calling of God in Christ Jesus."

Chapter Three

Life is the affirming

Text: Luke 11:14-28

"He that is not with me is against me"
(v. 23).

LIFE is a continuous search for affirmations.
The secret longing of every person is to find
something worth living *for*. Kierkegaard, the
Danish philosopher, lived in a state of despair
until he found something worth living for, something that he was willing to die for, something to
affirm.

We are constructed around a positive pole.
Life fulfills itself when it is positive affirmation.
The negative life, by going counter to this fact,
disrupts itself, and shrivels and dies. Military
strategists say it this way: "The best defense is
a good offense."

In the mountainous western areas of our country there were a number of airplane crashes at
army air bases erected during the war. Many of

these crashes were unexplainable, until it was discovered that a plane requires something upon which to rest its wings in its flight. It *depends* upon the body of air in which it is flying. So when it happened that a plane entered a pocket, a "vacuum," where there was no air, no up-draft against which its wings could rest, it crashed. An airplane cannot fly in a vacuum.

Large parts of the world, and of our world's thinking, seem to be caught in such a vacuum. The spectacle of Germany today should cause deep thought in all of us. Her problem, we are told, is that she is in a vacuum. She has no dominating ideology. Her people have been stripped of their faith in Hitler and have left—faith in nothing. She is fulfilling before our eyes the statement of her prophet, Nietzsche: "If we look long into the abyss, we shall find the abyss looking back into us." If she is to arise from the terrible plunge into nihilism, it must be on the wings of a positive, challenging faith. If she is to survive she must affirm.

All around us we see people floundering because they haven't found anything to give themselves to. A student comes to the last year of school and is asked, "What do you plan to do now?" and he replies, "I don't know; I haven't found what I want yet." And he drifts on. There is a need within him. It is a need for something to affirm. A G. I. returns from war and casts about in a state of indecision which dissipates all his time and energy. The high pitch of war is gone, and nothing has come in to match it in sustaining strength, nothing that he can affirm.

What we affirm will control our lives. We must affirm, or we will disintegrate. Institutions are filled with those who have lost their true selves because there has been nothing in their lives for them to affirm. Homes are filled with hypochondriac men and women who fritter away their days on meaningless odds and ends because there has never come to them any great affirmation. Without a great affirmation life is an empty thing, without center or direction. It is simply a collection of disassociated experiences, an eating and sleeping and toying with this and that as a person without appetite toys with his food.

Everyone wants something to live for. Here is where Jesus Christ meets our need. He lived positively. He affirmed Himself and His God so far that He could not deviate, even when His affirmation drove Him to the cross. In the light of the "adjustment" principle of modern psychology, this course was either fantastic or insane: Fantastic or insane, the world has not yet encountered anything which equals, for sheer sustaining strength, the belief in this crucified Savior.

Jesus offers to us His own strengthening faith. He who met sickness with health, blindness with sight, physical defects with soundness of limb, sin with forgiveness, evil with good, death with life, offers to us the same positive faith by which He lived.

Jesus' difficulty with the Pharisees was that their program was negative and His was positive; there was no room for theirs when His came in. The Pharisees were negative people, chronic kickers, fault-finders, heresy-hunters; and such folk have nothing to give to life. Jesus disturbed them because He offered a life of affirmation—faith in God, in man.

In our text, Jesus is confronted with a serious charge. He was in league, said His accusers, with the devil. He was casting out devils through the chief of the devils. That was how He performed those wonderful deeds. Jesus' reply is a masterful use of logic. It was, in effect, "If this is true, Satan is already defeated." Could Satan be fighting against himself? No—it is God who is fighting him, because God is positive goodness.

Life is lived in the positive, the affirmative mood. But most men are timid. Instinctively they are afraid of following too far any one program which is not proved to them before they begin. That is why they are not definitely and consistently on the side of God in their living. Such men make of their lives a civil war—they are constantly fighting themselves, and are being destroyed in the process. Their conscience tells them one thing, expedience another. And they wonder why it is that some Christians can be happy!

There is the man in business, for example. He wants two things. He wants a good business, and a good life. It may even be that he sincerely wants them both. He is confronted by the fact of Christ, and recognizes its valid claim upon his allegiance. But he can't affirm this fact wholeheartedly, because there is the matter of business to consider. There are certain customers, potential and actual, who are not wholehearted Christians, and whose business he might lose if he were. So he plays it safe. He cuts a few corners here and there to remain in their good graces. Business is good, but life is miserable. The reason? He is not affirming anything. Or rather, he is affirming a policy of business first and it is not enough.

There is the young person. He wants happiness, and he wants it badly. He sees dimly that happiness is possible in the Christian life, but realizes that the price is complete surrender to Christ, which means affirming certain ways of life to which he would rather not commit himself. So he goes his own way, finding pleasure. Occasionally he will ask a weak question—can we be Christian and do such and so? This poor person is carrying around only the vestiges of a conscience. Happy? No, not even while having a "whale of a good time." He has not affirmed.

Then there is another type of person. He is a

very commendable person, too. He has eliminated from his life all bad practices. He does not use
narcotics or alcohol, he does not indulge in profanity, he does not transgress the sixth command-
ment. He works hard. He has swept his house
clean. There is no flaw. But wait—perhaps there
is a flaw. Jesus said something about the folly of
sweeping one's house clean, and not putting anything good back. There is the flaw. This fine person has eliminated outward sin, which is excellent. But therein lies his entire program. He
thinks of Christianity only in these negative terms,
and that is not Christianity. It is only one of its
by-products. He has said, "No," to the right
things, but he has not yet said, "Yes," to anything. Love has not entered. He judges his
brother, instead of trying to win him. He con-
demns him instead of helping him. He has not
affirmed.

There was once a young man, you will remember, who swept his house clean of everything evil;
yet the absence of one positive good worked to
the ruin of his life. He thought he had done
enough; he would not do more; he would not
sell all and follow Jesus. He demonstrated the
truth of our text: "He that is not with me is
against me."

There are those who would like to run a
church, too, in such a negative way. Just keep it
going. Give just enough to meet the minimum re-

quirements. Don't try anything which might tax
our pocketbooks, or our energy, or our faithful-
ness. Have one service a week. That's enough.
Sing a few hymns, put a pittance in the collection
plate, slip out to a big Sunday dinner, and let life
roll merrily along until next Sunday, when we
shall do it all over again. But that is not a church.
A church is a positive affirmation, that God is
good and Jesus Christ is right. It stands with its
spire pointing heavenward, verifying the reality
of God. Its bell rings, summoning men to par-
take of that reality. If it does not affirm, by positive, yes, by reckless action, it has failed in its
duty. If it does not affirm, that well-swept edifice
of convenient religious custom will crumble. It
will have ceased to be a church.

Life is the affirming. It is affirming the fact of
God. Somehow I cannot resist the poetry of
Browning. It is so contagious. He found a truth
to sing about, and he sang it out. "God's in His
heaven—All's right with the world!" he sang. Not
much logic there. Just an affirmation. But the
spirit can't quarrel with it, simply because it is
so positive. We are not asked to prove God. The
simplest child can do that. He is so obvious, so
evident. We are simply to embrace Him, to assume Him, and then to affirm Him. Affirm Him
by living Him. The man who was asked, "How
do you know there's a God?" and replied, "That's
easy; I talked with Him this morning," was on

the right road. So many are spending most of their waking moments proving Him, but it never gets them anywhere. They mire down. There is no uplift in their lives. The devil is a good debater too. He used pretty good logic, even with Jesus, but Jesus defeated him simply by affirming God. Dare to do it. Those beliefs you secretly entertain, those hopes you secretly harbor—take them out, and shout them to the skies. Sing them out with your hearts and your living, and God will become real. You will find God by affirming Him.

Life is affirming the fact of Christ—His life, His death, His resurrection. I could recommend several good books for any to read who might have doubts about Him, and the best one is the New Testament. But one can read these through, time and again, and summon all the logical arguments he wishes, and prove conclusively the reality of all the beliefs the Christian Church holds about Christ, and yet never be a Christian. Why? Because Christ is understood only when we come to the point where we affirm Him. I know a man who argued with himself about Jesus for years, secretly realizing it was all true, yet outwardly resisting. His life was stalemated. He got nowhere. Then one day he said simply, "I shall live assuming it is all true. I shall simply, within myself and as best I can in my outward life, affirm Jesus." And the matter was settled. He found Jesus by affirming Him. And Jesus has revealed

Himself to this man increasingly from year to year. Oh, that we could get out of ourselves, out of our shells, and simply dare to affirm Jesus! It may seem a risk, but that is the only way anything worth while was ever grasped. It is the only way we can find Jesus!

Life is the affirming of the program of Christ. Here is the hardest test of all. To dare to be humble, to dare to be forgiving, to dare to walk the second mile, to dare to pray for somebody we do not like, to dare to share, to dare to give one-tenth of our income to His work, to dare to conduct our lives of public service in accordance with His program, to dare to stand up for cleanness in public morals, to dare to be loving. Here is where most of us break down: we fail to affirm with a life of Christian service. We affirm the fact of God and we find reassurance; we affirm the death and the resurrection and the blood atonement of Christ and we find peace of conscience; but if we fail to affirm with a life of Christian service we bottle up all the sunshine of these blessings which we have found. The life of Christian service is the proof of these blessings. The only way to prove that God loves us in Christ Jesus is to permit ourselves to be used by Him in the service of our fellows.

What couldn't happen if your congregation, to a man, would adopt the program of Christ and try to prove in daily living that Christ was right?

You would become a working force in the Kingdom, rather than the pastor's field for cultivation.
You would be too much for your community and
would have to spill out into much larger fields.

Have you affirmed your secret faith? Have you
taken it out of its closet and exposed it to public
opinion and the scrutiny of your neighbors? It is
the only way your secret faith will survive.

Are you living for, or against, or are you living
neutrally? Nobody can really live *neutrally,* and
nobody can live long merely being *against.* Life
is meant to be lived *for,* and this means for Jesus,
our Lord. If we are to be filled with the fullness
of Christ, we must embrace Him on His grounds,
and affirm Him according to His own words.

Chapter Four

Life is the sharing

Text: John 6:1-15

"And when Jesus had given thanks, he distributed to the disciples, and the disciples to them that were seated" (v. 11).

LIFE is interdependent. Nobody lives by himself alone. In reality there is no such person as a "self-made man." Consider the many forces which go into the formation of our personalities. Home, parents, school, family, neighborhood, community, have all left their stamp upon us. None of us has come up life's pathway alone. There have been the kind loans in periods of distress, the friendly advice in perplexing moments, the helping hand when the road became too difficult. At some time or other, every one of us has shared the goodness of somebody else. And who can number the prayers of which we know nothing which have carried us over hard places, and given us strength for living?

Life is meant to be interdependent. It is no accident. God, in His creative wisdom, did not bestow all of His gifts on any one person. His gifts were intended to complement each other, to develop each other. I have some gifts others do not have; others have gifts I do not have. I could go my single way, they could go their single ways; but we would all lose in the process.

Some gifts are not even put to use, realized as gifts, except as they are used together. A great choir is made, not from solo voices, but from voices which are meant to be shared, voices which have a blending quality. Out of the blended voices is created a tone of beauty.

When a person tries to monopolize something, we instinctively shrug him off. We have no respect for a giant business firm which becomes a monopoly, because it does this at the expense of somebody else. We do not enjoy people who monopolize the conversation, who monopolize our time and energy, because they do so at our expense. A business firm prospers as it keeps the good will of its public. To keep this good will, it must share something—either service, or quality of merchandise. If the system of private enterprise is going to continue, it must reckon with this factor. Life is the sharing.

Every community is a picture of joint living. Any organization which tries to dominate ceases to serve. Business, school, church—as they share, they grow together.

When we ask somebody to take a position of public trust, we say to him in effect, "You have something which we need, some gift which the community needs for its growth." Moreover, this man needs to share his gift if he is to grow too.

The plant world illustrates this interdependence of life beautifully. A seed has the qualities of life within itself, but it will never grow unless it is placed in the proper environment. There must be water; there must be soil; there must be air; there must be sun. When the seed becomes a plant we say, "Just think. All of this came from that small seed." But it did not. The various properties of nature shared in its growth.

Consider the body. The stomach does not say to the heart, "I want all the credit for the operation of this body." The heart and the lungs and all the other organs share in its operation, and the result is what we call good health.

Our civilization depends upon the principle of sharing. We are able to live as we do because there are tillers of the soil producing our food; because there are craftsmen using metal and wood to produce our implements; because there are service men keeping our modern conveniences in operation; because there are jobbers selling to us their goods; because there are doctors to heal; and teachers to instruct; and churches to ennoble. Life is the sharing. Let just one of these groups withdraw its service (today we call this a strike), and the normal flow of life stops. Life is the sharing.

If we share, then, we benefit—but there is a much greater reason than this for sharing. God shares with us His love, His strength, His power, His wisdom—Himself. The heathen can shiver with fear of their gods who, they believe, rule all of life according to whim. We Christians worship a God who first loved us, a God who was not ashamed of coming to us and walking with us, a God who left His throne to share our way of life, even to the extent of the cross. Therein God, by revealing His basic nature, has revealed the true nature of life.

To share because life is made that way is simply to say that it is expedient, that we must share to save our hides. Even though true, this is not a high enough motive. Yet how many there are who give a small contribution to the Community Chest and assume that they have thereby "shared." No. Life is the sharing for the Christian, not because it is expedient, but because it is Christ-like. Because God has shared Himself with us in Jesus, we share ourselves and others for Jesus. "We love because He first loved us."

How difficult it is to keep sight of this higher goal. We are too much like the disciples on the sunny afternoon of our text, who, as they saw 5,000 hungry persons, felt totally incapable of helping them, even if they wished to. And the text does not say that they really wished to! We look out over our world and see the gaping mouths, and say in all truthfulness, "There is so little I can do," and commiserate with the unfortunates, and do nothing. Plenty of tears are shared, but our world needs a sharing of food, and money, and time, and energy, and prayer.

There surely can be nobody who does not know that in Europe tens of millions are starving and freezing in a squalor which beggars description. We are all aware of the fact that in China and India famine slays millions each year, and leaves an even larger toll in pestilence, to say nothing of the needy at our doorsteps.

But we, like Philip, say, "Not even many times what I have can do anything about it, Lord, even though I'd like to help." Ah—we reckon without our Lord! Jesus asked, "How much do you have?" and made five loaves and two fishes more than enough. Even today, somehow, the gift which is entrusted to Him becomes many times larger than we realize. During the war years, our church had only one medical missionary in China—the only one for eight million people. One! Hopeless, we would say; utterly hopeless. But his life was entrusted to Jesus, and the work he performed staggers our imagination. Consider Grenfell in Labrador—alone in that wasteland. Yet his life reads like fiction, because he entrusted what he had to Jesus. One man may not loom very large in a community dominated by vice, but one man committed to Christ has been known more than once

to eliminate vice from whole cities and states. My
five dollar bill is pretty puny over against the tens
of millions needed for the rehabilitation of our
world; and yet, from somewhere there come many
more fives, and the goal is reached. Give Jesus
what you have, and its added effectiveness will
startle you.

But then, comes the rejoinder, people are so
unappreciative. One hates to give his hard-earned
money to people who don't even say, "Thank
you." We'd rather, then, keep it and give it where
it counts, we say. Well, there were five thousand
persons present that day. I can just hear them
saying that Jesus was certainly a wonderful Man
for providing this fine food. But I can also hear
them a short while later, crying and screaming,
"Crucify Him!" Jesus knew this would happen,
and still He gave. At one time, ten lepers came
to Him to be healed, you remember. Only one
showed appreciation. Did Jesus recall His gift
from the other nine? Did He say the next time
need confronted Him, "I won't give, because the
last time I gave nobody said 'Thank you' "?

Life is the sharing, not that we might share the
thanks, but that we might share Jesus Christ. A
man of limited income gave a poor stranger a
generous gift of cash. The surprised man asked
why he was doing that. "Because I have to show
and share the love of Christ within me," he said.
The Christian is the heart of the world, regard-

less of his financial condition. He sees the world's need, and meets it, asking no questions, because that is what Christ did for him.

But how true is the statement, "We have to take care of ourselves, because nobody else will"? "Everybody has to take care of himself," is the language of all too many. Oh, they may never say it; but their deeds speak for them.

Let us make an examination. Just a few days ago, a man remarked, "It is significant that we in the Midwest, the breadbasket of the world, have been spared—and not only spared, but have prospered in an unprecedented way during the war and post-war years." This *is* significant. But *why* have we prospered? Was it so that we could eat all we wished, while others were starving? Was it so that we could fill our own bins for our own future, disregarding the others? No. The world is built with a sense of balance, and we here were given the opportunity of topping the scales so the less fortunate might be helped. Men did make money during the war. Farmers have never lived so comfortably. And now today we face our choice: we can either give our money away, or have it taken from us through inflation. It is quite clear it was not all meant to remain here.

Is it true that we must, in that spirit, take care of ourselves—in the spirit which sees our own need, to the exclusion of all others? Jesus once said, "Consider the lilies . . . they spin not; yet your heavenly Father careth for them." Now, He was either right or wrong. Life was either meant to be shared recklessly in His plan of things, or it was not. He said it was. Yet so many of us (even good church people!) by our actions set ourselves over against Him and refute His words. When we do this, we have pronounced judgment upon ourselves. For as we share we live. As we share we discover the bountiful providence of God. But to refuse to share! Judgment is inherent in such a choice, for he who chooses to live *for* himself must live *by* himself.

Many times five thousand are awaiting the touch of Jesus upon your gift and mine. Perhaps that gift is our money, our goods—which go far. But perhaps that gift is ourselves. Let us place ourselves, then, in His hand, praying that He will use us, that we may be "cast out upon humanity's waters" for the bringing of the Bread of Life to all men.

Life is the obeying

Text: Luke 1:26-38

"And Mary said, . . . be it unto me according to thy word" (v. 38).

TWO men were returning from a walk one day. As they drew near the door to the house, one stopped, and with his cane pointed to the threshold of the open door. Looking at his friend he asked, "Can you step over that threshold?" "Of course," was the rather impatient reply. "You are that close to being a Christian," he told him.

We could reverse the story. With one step we can go through this door and leave this house. We are that close to losing our Christian faith.

The door to the Kingdom, then, is a swinging door. It swings in either direction. We can go in, or we can go out. Once we have gone in, it does not lock behind us. If we are outside, it has not locked in our faces.

Two men may go through life together. They have the same equipment. In mental ability and in personality there is little difference between

them. They know the same God, read the same
Bible, attend the same church, and hold to the
same religious truths. One makes a positive impact upon life, leaving his mark unmistakably,
radiating confidence and faith. His faith has
gripped him and claimed him. The other is a
fine fellow, but makes no great impression. One
fact separates them. There is a door which the
one has entered, and which the other is still pondering. This door is labelled "obedience."

Mary, the mother of our Lord, crossed this
threshold. Therein lies the secret to the understanding of her character. After the glorious pro-
nouncement of the angel, she summed up her entire life philosophy in the words, "Be it unto me
according to Thy word." She was submissive to
the divine will for her life. She discovered that
the key to the God-life is obedience. Life is the
obeying—obeying God.

Obedience is the door to faith. It is the threshold which all must cross if they are to get even a
glimpse of the great wonders of the Christian life.
Yet so many miss this door. Other doors seem so
obvious, such as the door of understanding. It
seems so logical to assume that if we can cross the
threshold of understanding, we shall have arrived.
In this frame of mind it is easy to assume that if
we can only understand this or that Scripture pas-
sage, we shall then be Christians; if we can speak
knowingly of theological things, we shall be Chris-

tians. But the world contains many who have entered the door of understanding, who still have not discovered the peculiar secret of the Christian life.

There are other doors, too, such as the door of "churchism." The reasoning here is, If we attend the church service and enter the spirit of its worship, we shall have the secret. But each Sunday our churches are filled with many who have entered this door, who are still lacking in spiritual force. There remains another door, the door of obedience.

It seems that every effort on the part of God is to bring us to that point where we can say, "Thy will be done." Even when He reasons with us, He may attack our human understanding of Him. Life never finds itself in His scheme of things until it gives in to His will. All the squirming and the twisting we witness in others and recognize within ourselves is simply a desperate effort to escape the door of obedience. The greatness of Mary is not only that she was *chosen;* she was *willing.*

Jesus saw the will of God for His life quite clearly, but the epic struggles in His life around which we rally our faith are those in which He demonstrated His willingness to be obedient. He could have seen the will of God and taught us the principle of the cross and been a great teacher. But He saw the will of God and went through with the ordeal of the cross, and became our Savior. He has taught us evermore that life is the obeying.

So many people have missed this very simple truth. They stand just outside the door. They know they "ought" to do this or that, and the fact that they don't appears to cause them great concern. They "ought" to pray, to attend church services, to make up with their neighbor, to stop cursing or drinking. They know this so well they tell others about it. They see what they must do, but *will not* do it. What they "ought" to do hovers over them as a dread shadow, clouding their souls. It is the door of obedience they dread.

Sometimes it appears that such people are waiting for a near miracle to change them. If only a catastrophe would crop up in their lives, then perhaps they would do what they "ought" to do. So they reason with themselves. They have heard it taught that we cannot even believe in God by ourselves, that the whole Christian life, and especially faith, is a gift of God by the Holy Spirit. Perhaps they choose to believe this in the wrong sense, thus enabling them to blame God for their lack. So they decide to play a waiting game, waiting for God through the Spirit to convince them. Thus they live, with the greatness of the Christian life continuing to elude them. At times it toys with them. They sense the fullness which is lying at their fingertips, if they can but bring themselves to say, "I will." But the strength to say this never comes. So they continue, waiting, for some overwhelming experience, some overwhelming argument which shall press them down until they cannot help themselves, and shall be compelled to say, "Be it unto me as Thou wilt." But the moment never comes. They continue to live in the shadows, missing the greatness of life with Christ, because God doesn't work that way. He does not make puppets of us, saying in an indulgent tone, "Now you must cross this threshold." It is we who must take that step. Obedience requires effort on our part. Life is the obeying.

Now it is a fact that the obedient one is often unnoticed, shunted to the sidelines of life. He is often unspectacular; but he is always heroic. He may pass by unnoticed, but he is always in the thick of the battle. Many a soldier who never won a decoration actually possessed the true qualities of bravery. Many a man who talked with bravado of patriotism didn't lift a patriotic finger during the war. Many a man who talked of his great courage, failed in the pinch; and many a quiet, unnoticed boy rose to great heights because unquestioningly he did his task. He rose to the occasion. Why? Because he was obedient. In obedience lay the test of patriotism and true courage.

It is often that way in the Christian life too. We notice the spectacular one while all the time there is another one going quietly on his way, who is really bearing the brunt of the battle. He has been obedient. He has enough of spiritual understanding to recognize the voice of God; and hearing it, he obeys. Faith is as simple, and as difficult, as that.

Jesus once told a simple story of two boys. Both were asked by their father to do the same task. One said, effusively, "I will," but didn't. The other rebelled and said "No," but later did it. And it was the one who finally obeyed who was demonstrating the principle of obedience as the gateway to the Kingdom of God.

"I am perfectly willing to obey," you may say, "but I don't seem to be able to figure out what God's will is." Many a well-meaning one has been caught in this predicament. At times God's will does seem obscure. But this statement is too often merely an evasion.

God's will is not really so difficult to recognize. It is always on the side of moral right. Adultery is wrong. Dishonesty is wrong. Profanity is wrong. It is utterly impossible to hold that these might under any situation be right. It is God's will that these be shunned in our daily living. Kindness to our fellow men is His will. Self-sacrifice, service, honest and moral living—these are the will of God. Only a casual perusal of the Bible would reveal that to anybody. Now the person who is interested in doing the will of God must begin there. He begins there by obeying. In so doing, he is on the highroad to faith.

If you are to do God's will you must eliminate every habit which interferes with His working in you, regardless of what that habit is. It may be working on the Sabbath, or simply sleeping late. It may be all those card parties which sap your time, energy, and money. It may be one of a hundred things; you know yourself what it is. If you are really concerned with knowing His will, you may be certain it begins there. You cannot expect to understand God or His will until you are willing to begin by obeying, and by obeying where you are now rebelling.

God's will is always that you be more generous, more forgiving, more prayerful, more worshipful. These are attributes you discover by doing, not by reasoning. Life is the obeying.

God's will is that you enter His service, as full-time worker or as consecrated layman. We are called into His vineyard to be laborers. You were *intended* to teach Sunday school, to be a personal witness for Jesus Christ, to serve in your Church through its organizations. That is in the scheme of things. But so many stand on the wrong side of the door arguing with their conscience, professing to be puzzled by some religious truth, while the fact is that all the time there is one truth which they are evading—the truth that they ought to obey God rather than men. Life is the obeying.

We grow in Christ very much in this way: First, we are baptized. God's powerful grace has become a working part of us. Secondly, we are taught. We are schooled in the way of salvation. We are brought, by patient teaching, to a knowledge of at least the rudiments of faith. This brings us right up to the threshold of the door of obedience. The next step is that we simply will to do what God wants, that we will to be what God has always intended. There is the difficult, almost insurmountable obstacle. Rationalizing, logic, everything, rushes to our rescue, making it so easy to be content with a sacrament and our knowledge.

The peculiar fact is that once you enter this door of obedience, other doors open up too. This is so because through obedience we come into the very heart and center of Christian living. The most simple men have been known to become great Bible teachers, and even greater souls, because they were obedient. Life is the obeying.

If you stand in a shaky spot, simply do this. Find the most obvious requirement of God upon your life which you are trying to avoid, and then obey. Obey even if it means surrendering your most enjoyable habit or possession or trend of thought. If it is causing you double living and thinking, it is not worth the keeping. Give it up. If it is some particularly distasteful work, do it. That is what we mean by surrendering to Jesus.

And then something will happen. The failure to take this step of surrender is what keeps so many out of the Kingdom. Once this little step has been taken, the beauty of the whole realm of the Kingdom is unfolded, and we marvel that we hesitated so long. We grasp the meaning of forgiveness, and of brotherly love, and of eternity. And in addition to this spiritual understanding, we receive that other great blessing, spiritual strength. But the key to such understanding, such strength, is obedience.

"What is God's will for all men?" is the first question in our catechism. The answer—"It is God's will that all men be saved and come to a knowledge of the truth."

Now His will for us is really our will for ourselves, too, is it not? We want to be "saved," all of us. We want it—He wishes it. Where, then, is our difficulty? It is simply that we want it on our own terms, whereas it is obtained only on God's terms. God's terms are—the cross. Jesus, our Savior, in whom God's will and ours meet, had to meet those terms. Even He had to "learn obedience." He obeyed—even when obedience drained His life blood, in the garden and on the cross—that you and I might be able to meet God's terms. Our obedience lies in our willingness to accept that cross, as our payment for sin, and our taskmaster for life. "Take up thy cross." Life is the obeying.

Chapter Six

Life is the witnessing

Text: Matthew 21:1-9

"All the city was moved, saying, Who is this? And the multitude said, This is Jesus" (vv. 10, 11).

A SALES manager of a large company was addressing his final remarks to his sales force. He had described in detail the company's product, pointing out its strong points, the points on which it surpassed its competing products, and had arrived at the final conclusion that it was the superlative product in its field. Addressing the men, he asked, "Do you see this?" All nodded their heads. Then, with keen insight, he asked "Do you believe this is true?" That man knew human nature. It is hard to sell something on which you are not sold yourself.

A student who had been having great difficulty with his speech course was assigned a rather drab topic. The instructor had just about become convinced that he was hopeless in the field of public speaking. But it happened that this particular topic was one on which he felt keenly. His talk was a shock, because of the warmth of its presentation, its clear, concise development. The instructor watched him keenly, then remarked to the class, "Life is more than the mechanics. It requires convictions." We must be able to witness to something honestly to be effective.

There is a great difference between knowing something "by heart" and knowing it "from the heart." Rote knowledge never helped anyone. It cannot witness. The scribes of the day of Jesus knew their religion "by heart." They could rattle off religious arguments without any pains. The disciples of Jesus knew their religion from the heart. They may not have been glib, but they were profound, profound because of an inner experience. As such they were convincing.

This difference in approach to life is a deep-seated one. It is basic to the problem of effective living, in every sphere. If a politician knows only the mechanics of politics, he remains a politician, but if he feels the needs of his country, the problems of his day, the right and the wrong, he becomes a statesman. He has become a witness. We say of a musician that he is mechanically perfect, but lifeless—or we say he is warm, that his music comes from within. One must be a witness to the place of music in one's life in order to be a mu-

sician. A man may know, like the scribes, all the
rudiments of religious knowledge, and be a theo-
logian. A man learns to know God through Jesus
—and becomes a Christian.

It is the witness who is the salt of the earth, the
light of the world. It is the witness who is the
heart of society, the cleansing blood stream of his
day.

It is the peculiar nature of Christianity that
its adherents are intended to be witnesses. Everything is directed to the end that we be witnesses.
So long as the Church is a witness, it is a power.
When it becomes a speculative affair, it is already
weak. So long as a man can witness to the power
of Christ, he is a leaven. When he becomes an
armchair philosopher, discoursing upon self-evi-
dent truths, he has lost his force.

Palm Sunday is a day of witnessing. Jesus rode
into the city in the midst of wide acclaim. Thou-
sands broke the silence with their shouts of "Ho-
sanna." He had captivated their enthusiasm. And
they expressed it with all the fervor of a people
long starved for a popular hero to adore.

But it was false witnessing. It was cheap,
thoughtless witnessing. The people knew some
facts, but these had not been burned into their
hearts and minds. They were surface impressions,
easily erased. How few there were who understood, who remained faithful in the days that followed, who walked to the cross! But the few who

did were witnesses, and their witness has remained until our day, winning, convincing. Consider John, for just one, and the impact of his
deep understanding of the heart of God, because
he permitted God to control his own heart.

There may be many witnesses of the Palm Sunday sort at the time a church is built. It may be
easy then to shout, "Now we'll show them. Now
we've got something!" How many remain? How
many through the years have the full meaning of
the church and its Savior burned ever deeper into
their beings? To what, in fact, does your church
testify in your own community? To an enthusiasm
gradually cooling? To a love diminishing with
the years? To worldliness? Or to lives being re-
made, ennobled? Our church can be a witness, too.

The early Church did something to its generation for one simple reason. It was a witnessing
church. It had a "message to tell to the nations."
So long as it had a message, and told it, it pro-
duced results. But then the inevitable happened.
Instead of witnessing, men began discussing. Instead of proclaiming, they began speculating. Instead of shouting the "good news," they began
arguing about its form. The result was: it grew
cold, formal, lifeless. At spasmodic intervals men
again arose and began to witness, and it was in
those periods that the Church marched.

Where are we? We are told that baptism used
to be a vital process, whereby one was marked;

hence the admonition to the sponsors, "In case of the death of the parents, to nurture the child in faith and piety." To be a Christian often meant death, hence baptism was a witnessing. Perhaps it is because it has ceased to be so vital, that we dress it up today into a beautiful, but too often meaningless, performance, worrying mostly about whether or not the baby will cry.

The Lord's Supper is marked with death. It is a crucial affair where we see that our own sin is of such consequence that we have to eat the broken body and blood of our Savior to atone for it. The intense longing of the heart after purity, the deep-seated fear of moral defeat, the breathless approach to a God who would dare to die—these are the Sacrament. With trembling hands we receive the body and blood—or do we? Is it possible we have lost its true meaning in our theological speculating? Is it witnessing to God's grace in Christ, or to theological opinions or to church customs, such as communion once a year to maintain membership? And what of attendance at worship? And what of our instruction of the young? Are they a witness or a procedure? Do they testify or stultify?

You see, Palm Sunday tells us that life is the witnessing. When the Pharisees asked Jesus to make His followers stop singing their songs of praise, Jesus remarked, "I tell you God would make these very stones shout if they should be still."

How much of our Christian living, and our feeble attempts at preaching, are just a sort of salad course, beautifully garnished, but with no sustaining value, because we do not really witness!

What, then, is a witness? A witness is more than an onlooker. He is more than a sight-seer, who has browsed upon the beauties of the Kingdom and then come home to report. It is possible to graze lightly in the Green Pastures, absorb a certain religious atmosphere and terminology, and become a scribe. This may seem to be witnessing, but the witnessing that settles things is of a different sort.

A witness is one who has nothing to lose. He is therefore an adventuresome sort, though he may not appear to be so. He has nothing to lose because of one simple fact—he has already lost all. Through an inner process he has gradually come to the point where he has lost himself and all that he is and has. He stands alone and naked—but "clothed upon." He has lost all, and gained all.

Who is this witness? He is one who has come to know the deep, tragic meaning of sin. He is one who has come to grips with his own futility.

He has tried everything, and it has all backfired. Nothing works. He worked long and hard to secure an education, in order that he might arrive at the top of the pile, but after he arrived, he had no more incentive for living. Everything became futile. Or, he worked arduously at amassing money in order that he might have old-age security, and then when old age came he found not security but a constant, gnawing fear. Not a fear of losing what he had, but a fear that he might not be what he thought he was. His very security became his futility, as it refused to assure his heart and comfort his spirit. Or, he played long and hard at having fun. When one pleasure wore out there was always another new one. So he went on and on, from one worn-out pleasure to the next, until all he had was a scrap-heap of burned out pleasures, and ashes where there should have been a heart.

Or, it may be that he took the matter of the good life seriously. Endowed with a strong will and practical common sense, he managed to escape moral pitfalls. He began to seek and to enjoy the title of "a respectable man, a good citizen." And yet—there was a worm eating away inside, reminding him that unless he could become in his heart what he appeared to be in his actions, his cloak of goodness would be his shroud.

Or he may simply have done what so many of us have done—lived from day to day, eating, sleeping, dreaming a dream, perhaps, but earth-bound. He wanted to live the good life, but never quite succeeded. So he began overlooking his small defeats, which only he knew about anyway. He was stalemated, beaten. So he became penitent. God said He would hear the cry of the penitent, didn't He? Each night he repented, and felt better, because certainly his penitence would beat down the walls of heaven! There was a certain comfort, but vague misgivings entered. Nevertheless he continued—repenting, but never growing. Life was a vicious circle, futile, meaningless. Has the sense of your own futility claimed you? Then realize that you are knocking at the gates of the Kingdom. You are nearer than you think. You are futile for one small, simple reason. You are clinging to something which is you—your prestige, your money, your sins, your character, your penitence.

What can be done about it? Is it a matter of simply trying something? What shall we try? A new hat, dress, suit, house, environment? So many have been brought this far, only to dissipate their opportunity by trying a change of scenery. We cannot run away from the futility of sin, nor can we rearrange our spiritual houses in any way that will crowd it out. No, it is a new self we need. We must try a new way, a new belief. We must try Him who said, "Whoso cometh to me I will in no wise cast out"; Him who said, "Come unto me, ye heavy-laden"; Him who said, "I and my Father are one"; Him who said, "Whosoever would save his life, must lose it, for my sake, and the Gospel's."

So, the next step is self-losing in Him. This is always an act of desperation, a throwing of self upon Him, come what may; an acceptance of forgiveness, come what may; a relying upon His guidance, come what may. If you do this, the Jesus I know will not let you down. He begins His work by giving something called "peace," a peace which is not just the absence of futility, but the presence of purpose; a peace which is not just an escape from guilt, but an entrance into spiritual reality. This peace acts as an inner dynamo. It spurs and drives, and gives a sense of well-being and confidence.

And so, under the creative hand of the Holy Spirit, a witness is born.

Having lost himself in self and found nothing, he loses himself in Christ and finds everything.

Have you lost yourself in Christ? Have you submitted to Him all those misgivings you have about yourself? Have you gone all the way and trusted in His way of salvation? Do not try to witness if you haven't. Or better yet, try it; it will be difficult to attest to something you only half believe. You will be tormented, until you let Christ move all the way in; when you do this, you will have few misgivings—you will have a fire, like Jeremiah felt, eating your inward parts, compelling you to testify.

God give us witnesses for our day, witnesses who can say with the sure word of experience, "Come to Jesus Christ. Try His way. It works. I tell you I know!"

Chapter Seven

Life is the risen Lord

Text: Mark 16:1-7

"Ye seek Jesus of Nazareth, which was crucified. He is risen. (v. 6).

EASTER is a day for anthems, not for arguments; for praises, not for polemics; for hallelujahs, not for learned discussions. The pondering, the discussing pro and con—these are prelude to Easter. When Easter visits the heart of a man, he ceases to speculate and begins to demonstrate. He ceases to wonder and starts to believe.

The language of the New Testament is not an "In memoriam," singing the praises of a great leader now gone. We celebrate the birthday of Lincoln and adulate his highmindedness and his superb political philosophy. But behind it all we know he is dead and will not return. So there remains only his greatness, now dead, and his philosophy, gone with him, which we frantically try to reclaim in our oratory. But we leave such memorial services with a sense of futility—"If there could only be another Lincoln." No, the New Testament is rather a "Te Deum." It is a simple declaration. It is contemporary. It tells us Jesus lives. His words have power. His teaching has impact. The New Testament is not so much a proof as a demonstration.

Consider for a moment that first Easter. A dejected group of disciples greeted the dawn that first Sunday 2,000 years ago. Their faces were drawn. They were listless, apathetic. They had followed Jesus so intimately, they had been so closely under His spell, that till now there had been time for little or nothing else. Life for them had been Jesus Christ, because He had given to them hope and faith. Now He was dead. They were like the little girl who lost her mother. A well-meaning lady said to her, "You have lost a wonderful mother." The sobbing girl said, almost angrily, "I have lost my home." Mother had been, actually, her entire life. The disciples had lost more than a Leader; they had lost their whole way of life.

But then the electrifying news came. "He is not dead. He is risen. The tomb is empty." Despair turned to doubt; doubt, to incredulous amazement; amazement, to action. Peter and John got to their feet and ran with all their might to see whether it was so. It was. Jesus had defeated death. Forty hectic days followed, days in which Jesus came to them to let them know He had arisen. Then came the day of Pentecost, when the Holy Spirit assured them with quiet conviction that Jesus was alive and with them.

What a transformation! A new life possessed them. They were driven now, not by an ardor such as they had felt when He was on earth because of His great deeds and wise words, but by a quiet confidence which gave power. It was the sure knowledge that Jesus was alive. It was this conviction which fired their missionary zeal and their preaching. Jesus lived, and because He lived, they were to continue living, and all men could also live if they would follow Him. This was the amazing story they had to tell, and which they simply *had* to tell. The pages of the New Testament reveal to us that life for the disciples and the early Christians was simply "The risen Lord." They went to pagan countries to state their case—not to argue, but to convince, to uplift, to give the same hope they had found, to tell all men that death was defeated. Here was One who had risen from the dead. Life was the risen Lord.

It is amazing what this testimony was able to do. Before learned men they found they were more wise. The resurrection had unlocked their minds and given them surpassing wisdom. For all human minds are locked in the fear of death. All human thinking is limited by death. But these men went beyond. Like Stephen, they literally beheld Jesus seated at the right hand of God. Their testimony was irrefutable. It was not the highly emotional testimony of some modern "isms." The fact that such learned men listened to them reveals this. It was a quiet, unshakable certainty. Jesus was risen, and this tremendous *fact* had changed the entire matter of living.

Paul, of course, said it best. After meeting the risen Christ, his life was changed. After living a score of years or more on the strength of this faith, he said, "I am crucified with Christ, nevertheless I live; yet not I, but Christ liveth in me." Or as he stated it more simply later on, "To me to live is Christ." His logic was: Christ lives. He lives in me by faith. I live. He even began to say this unconsciously. It slipped, almost unnoticed, into his conversation. Thus he could say one time, when discussing the future, "When He who is our life shall appear"—"He who is our life"— glorious fact!

How could Paul make such a statement? And what did he mean by it? Do you remember the night you sat at your desk writing your beloved a letter and looking at her picture in front of you? As you sat there you wrote, "You are my life." What did you mean?

You meant that she had given you a new life for an old one. You meant that her love was so meaningful that you lived in the strength of it.

And you meant that you would gladly do anything in your power for your beloved.

This may help us to understand what Paul meant and what every Christian means when he says, "To me to live is Christ."

Paul meant that Christ had actually given him a new life for an old one. There had been a trade. Paul had come with his old life of religious bigotry, self-righteousness, selfishness, pride, ambition, and given it to Jesus. Jesus had, in return, given him a life of brotherly love, humility, service, the forgiveness of sins. Paul could never forget that contrast between the old and the new. The new life, the Christ life, was so deeply satisfying that Paul's one fear thereafter was that he should lose it.

That is the only way in which the risen Christ can be operative in our lives. We enter His life only through this exchange method. Some are grafted into Him in youth and grow in Him so constantly that they never have that painful experience of a transfusion of new life. This is ideal. But mostly we become conscious of the risen Christ through the painful process of giving up the old for Him, either as a totally new experience or as a reclaiming of what we had in youth but had lost along the way.

For the Christian "to live is Christ," because of a throbbing awareness of the difference between the two. He gives us new life for old.

Paul meant also that Christ was the constant source of sustenance for this new life. For him to live was Christ because he lived in spiritual dependence upon Christ. We must take this literally. Life is the risen Lord not simply because His example challenges us and His teachings edify us, but because He who is life keeps us living.

The diabetic may say of his insulin, "This is my life." The man who suffers from anemia may say of the liver extract he must take into his system, "This is my life." The Christian, who was dead in sin but is now alive in Christ, says, "To me to live is Christ." Every Christian makes this discovery in the same way. He attempts, for a while, to live this new life on his own strength. Fired by the lofty idealism of the Christian faith, he lives the new life with zeal. But then comes the day when he realizes that his fire is dying down, that it becomes more and more of an effort to keep the faith. It is when this realization drives him to the point of living one day at a time, content with letting Jesus be his strength for each twenty-four hours of living, that he discovers the full and deep meaning of "To me to live is Christ."

For the Christian life is one of complete dependence upon the risen Lord. The Christian life always flounders when we separate its ethical and moral and idealistic teachings from their Author! Goodness must be personalized to be living. It is not necessarily true, as we are so prone to say, that right will always triumph, that love will conquer hate, that meekness will defeat force. It is only true because love is triumphant in Him, and holiness is personified in Him, for it is He who gives to the virtues of the Christian life their sustaining and their resurgent power. Because of Christ, the risen Christ, we can say that right will always triumph. Without the risen Christ, even the best intentions will miscarry. So we depend upon Him for the nourishing of the Christian life.

Furthermore, we must realize that the Gospel is a tremendous responsibility for our earthly vessels. We will, even the best of us, sometime or other prove untrue to our trust. Sin will have its day even in the reborn life. It is then that we see in its deepest implications that "to live is Christ." For when we are living a life which is not our own, and then lose that life, it is not in our power to reinstate it. We must come back to the source. He who gave it must resurrect it when we let it slip. "Thy sins are forgiven thee" is the life-restoring word. To that word we cling, with a desperation almost of fear, for it is in that word that we are cleansed, day by day. We live in the dependence of the sinner upon his Savior.

It is, in a sense, a borrowed life we are living. We can draw upon it without limit, but we must draw upon it, or we shall lose it. I like to imagine Paul as he said this. I can picture him, weak, worn out from his difficult life and exhausting work. He has sunk into his chair, wondering if he can continue. And then he remembers the promise, "My grace is sufficient for thee," and he turns again to his Lord in prayer and is received and refreshed. And I can see him rising with the same old light in his eyes, and saying, "To me to live is Christ."

Not only had Paul received a new life for an old one, and found that Christ was able to sustain it, he had now also found a purpose for living. Every new venture in his life became a venture on behalf of Christ.

Here is one of the great secrets of the Christian life. There will be just as much of the enabling grace of Christ in our lives as we are attempting things for Him. His sustenance is always equal to our undertakings, no more, no less. We need to exert ourselves to the extent that we are tackling something bigger than ourselves, if we are to experience this sustaining life of Christ.

We must begin at home. Christ is more than equal to that sin which so plagues us. But His grace moves in direct proportion to our efforts. He does not pluck the sins out of our lives as a gardener weeds his garden. But as we, with resolution, stand up against our own sins, He quietly moves in and equips us with a strength which is not our own. It is the same in any undertaking for Him. It makes no difference what the undertaking is, whether talking to others about Him, combatting wickedness in high places, or in spreading the Gospel, His sustaining grace is proportionate to our efforts.

"Ah," some will say, "but I have tried. I have fought and fought, and worked and worked, but always fail." Excellent. It is always that way, when we try in our own strength. But as we work in His strength, something happens. The failure is not only to be expected, it is a blessing. For it is in the very failure of our undertakings that we are driven deeper into Him, "who is our life."

Life is the risen Lord. Has Easter visited us with this victorious result? We have cause to wonder.

In too many places we have become a church on the defensive. We have been apologizing for our faith. We have been engaged in defending our position, and in making it reasonable to a skeptical world. Our faith is becoming ingrown. We are wandering about within ourselves in search of proofs. We are looking through the history books in search of reasonable arguments. And not very much is happening!

The simple truth is this: if our faith is of such a calibre that we need to search through libraries to bolster it, it is not worth having! If our Christian faith is of the kind that we must be apologetic about, why retain it? The Christian faith was intended to be wings, not a weight. I can not imagine the disciples going about arguing, proving

why Jesus' statements were true. They would
have gained a hearing doing that, of course. But
the significant fact is that this is not at all what
they did. They said simply, "Jesus Christ is risen
from the dead. Follow Him." The fact of His
rising lent power to His teachings, His teachings
became living, and the whole became one powerful fact. Life is the risen Christ.

Likewise, if I, or any preacher, should ask you
to accept a belief which had so little to commend
it that you would have to spend the rest of your
days bolstering it by straw arguments, we would
be merely a drain upon you and your time. But
we have something else to say. It is simply, "Jesus
is living today, and because He is, life is the risen
Lord." We have the high privilege of proclaiming
to you an incomparable message, and of assuring
you that if you follow His advice of proving Him
by trying Him, you have a rare discovery in store
for you. For you too will receive a new life for
your old one, a life of transcendent worth and
happiness.

Is Christ the source of our life as Christians
and as a Church, without whom our days are
lusterless and heavy? Or has He become a peg on
which we hang our theological thinking? Or
worse yet, a piece of bric-a-brac which we keep
safely on the corner shelf, being careful not to
damage it, only seeing to it that it is dusted and
polished each Sunday?

"But now is Christ Jesus risen from the dead." This is the bald and simple fact of Easter. But it is not an isolated fact. It is a fact which has reached into every nook and cranny of life. To remove it and to look at the fact of the resurrection in isolation is like trying to take out the center piece of an intricate puzzle. It cannot be done without upsetting the entire puzzle.

But because He is risen we can know that His way is the living way. Because He is risen we can know that kindness is stronger than cruelty; right than wrong; meekness than force; humility than arrogance; forgiveness than vindictiveness. He staked this faith on the cross. And He arose. From henceforth all who trust in Him can also walk in newness of life.

Is this the fact which dominates your life? Do you literally live because Christ lives? Or do you merely admire His philosophy? Do you live your life, knowing somewhat casually that Christ arose —a fact we remember at Easter—and when we die we shall live, if we are good? Believe me, that will not happen, unless in this life we live because He lives.

Perhaps we fail because we do not really test the Christian life. There is only one way to test it. That is to live, in all respects, as if it were actually true that Christ is alive.

Will you do this? For one week only, or for one day only, consciously exercise this faith you have by living deliberately as if Christ were living and present. Such days will be different!

In the first place, we will have the consciousness of being under His constant gaze. That changes a good many things we do and say, does it not?

In the second place, we will have the realization of being in constant debt to His forgiveness and mercy. That alters a good many opinions we have of ourselves, does it not?

In the third place, there will be a holy impatience in us to be rid of the partition between Him and us and come into His presence, that we may see Him more clearly and hear Him more correctly.

Christ is the risen Lord. God give us grace to live as if we believed it to be true!

Come

MIDWEEK MEDITATIONS FOR LENT

Chapter Eight

Come

Text: Revelation 22:17

"And the Spirit and the bride say, Come. And let him that heareth say, Come. And let him that is athirst come."

THE world today is a dissonant medley of voices. It is difficult, in the confusion caused by a thousand and one calls to spiritual allegiance, for the average man to give a response, to make a decision. It is as if we stood on a huge entertainment midway, with men everywhere inviting us to come and try their wares. The golden trumpets calling for followers and the silver tongues asking allegiance have become so numerous that Christ's prophecy, "There shall arise false prophets, saying, 'See here is the Christ, and here, and there,'" has become frighteningly real.

There is the voice of the church, the fraternal organizations, the trade and business groups, the health clubs, political parties, political idealogies. Each in turn is subdivided, with each subdivision clamoring loudly for a hearing.

We are a generation distracted. In our secret

selves there has come the unconscious admission that we are lost, that there must be some voice with supreme authority, but we cannot find it! Our political, our social, our religious goals are so intertwined; the spokesmen for each sound so alarmingly similar in purpose. One man tells you to rear your children by the new psychology; that is to say, "Let them do what they please." Another tells you to use the rod. One voice proclaims Russia, and still another America, as the champion of individual rights, and even of God. We follow one voice for a while, then another, but they lead us to dead-end streets, where there is no turning, no light. We are a generation disillusioned.

H. G. Wells tells the story of a man who dared to brave the terrors of a haunted house. At first, he was very brave indeed; but the unnatural noises, the squeaks, and the groans soon undermined his confidence. Finally, he entered a room where he saw a row of candles burning on a table, and to his horror watched these candles being snuffed out, one by one, by an unseen hand. We are, in our generation, in a similar situation. Our house is haunted and, one by one, we have witnessed the snuffing out of those lights we had planned to follow, the extinguishing of those values to which we had attached our hopes. We are alone in the dark.

Of course, the snuffing of these candles is a

blessing, but this is so hard to see. Some of the bankruptcy of ideals which faces us is a wholesome bankruptcy of superficial and complacent idealism. Some men who followed the way of science have been finally filled only with dismay. Some who have scrambled after material possessions have found that such a course stifles the soul. Yes, the defeat of some of our fondest hopes has opened our ears to the call of God. His is the only force which can tie up these loose ends, mould together the broken pieces, and bring order and purpose and direction into lost lives. Up to us, then, to keep our ears tuned, our spirits responsive to His call. Up to us to keep peace, to cease our foolish clamoring, and to listen to His call, as He pleads with us, inviting us to accept His grace in Jesus Christ.

Now, just what constitutes His call? He said so many things to us. His Word is replete with admonitions, urgings, pleadings, invitations. Numerous voices are busy telling us that the great word in God's vocabulary is "Do." We are reminded that there is much to do, and that we must be busy with His business. Their text is, "By their fruits ye shall know them." And, of course, this is valuable advice. We are all too lazy spiritually. . . . Then we are told forcibly that God's wording is mostly "Don't," and His "Thou shalt not's" are forced upon us constantly. This, too, is needful. We are all too weak and self-centered. . . . Again, we are told that His language, His key word is "Go"; that we are to be witnesses for Him; that missionary-mindedness is the clue to the Christian life. This, too, is something our arm-chair religion needs to hear. . . . Somebody else tells us that the word is "faith." Another says the word is "Church." Still another says the word is "prayer."

But to emphasize any of these *first* is a mistake. To *emphasize* these is to misunderstand God's prime intention, and in fact, God Himself, in the light of Scripture. In the midst of darkness, dissonance, confusion, there is one clear voice. "Come," He says. "Come." God, standing at the gateway to an Eden forfeited, and calling, "Adam, where art thou?"—That is God. God in the stillness of the night interrupting Samuel's sleep. —That is God. Jesus standing at the crossroads, saying, "Come unto me."—That is God. God stooping down to our level and saying with infinite patience, "Come, let us reason together. Though your sins be as scarlet."—That is God.

The Gospel is not an admonition; it is an invitation. It tells us that God may be a judge, but He is primarily a host. He loves justice, but His mercy and love *are* His justice. Isn't that the voice our generation is actually sick to hear? Isn't it the voice that offers forgiveness of our sins, whether we have repressed them, confessed them, or actually chosen them? Come, COME!

When it comes down to the last analysis, it is this "Come" which is the great stumbling stone for so many. It is not the "Do," the "Don't," the "Go" which bother, so much as it is the "Come." We are legalists by inheritance. We rather like to work under orders. We are addicts of rote, and order, and law. No, the big problem for the human mind is not the command; it is the invitation. It is the word "Come." We are a little skeptical of it. It is too simple. There must be something else, something which we can *do*.

But the Gospel is God in invitation—nothing more, nothing less. A mother was putting her rebellious son to bed. This night the mother was in good spirits. The little one cried and cried. He didn't want to go to bed. But the mother laughed, and as she undressed him she gave him a hug. "Even when you cry and are naughty, I like you," she said. The boy was startled, startled out of his tears. Something was wrong here. So he tried again, stamping his feet for emphasis. But she repeated it, "No matter how bad you act, I still love you." The boy regarded her with thoughtful eyes. Suddenly quiet, he put his arms around her neck, and said fervently, "I love you, too, mommy."

That is the Gospel. That is the heart of God. Life doesn't begin until this unfathomable love has startled us out of our rebellion. We are still in the dark until that whisper, "Come, sinner—my blood is sufficient," has placed us in the light. So

that is all there is to it, after all. The preachers
were right then. The Sunday school teacher was
right, and my parents. God is love, and what a
mighty love! The only call which can answer
life's baffling problems has been heard and heeded.

> "I heard Him call,
> 'Come, follow.' That was all.
> My gold grew dim,
> My soul went after Him,
> I rose and followed.
> That was all.
> Who would not follow
> If he heard Him call?"

Have you listened to this call? Of course you
have heard it. Hardly anybody within reach of
these words can say he hasn't heard that call. But
have you listened? And have you come?

So many think, "This is just a religious technique, perfected by masters of mass psychology."
And they go their way with a sneer. Others,
good church people, think, "This is for the un-
converted. I have come." Both are wrong. It is no
technique. The artless simplicity of it offends
their own double-mindedness, where there is
often a hidden purpose behind each display of
friendship. Listen to the testimony of the countless—and you certainly know at least one of them
—who have found life and peace by taking God at

His word and following the invitation. And make no mistake. Don't think that you come once, and then are rid of this voice. In fact, they who have heard its deep, forgiving tones, are the very ones who never seem to get enough of it. The uniqueness of Jesus Christ is that He must always be out in front. As a sheep is lost when it loses its shepherd, so are we when we get out of earshot of that voice. We live purely in response to that "Come." He calls us here. He calls us there. He calls us to still deeper repentance, to still higher consecration. We don't come just once, but daily. Pity the man whose coming occurred in some dim yesterday, and from which he has gained no more satisfaction.

The trouble with most of us is that we have never come far enough. Some, like the rich young ruler and King Felix, have come out of curiosity. But that is not far enough. Still others, like Judas Iscariot, have come out of selfish interests, but that is not far enough. We must come all the way. That means—to the foot of the cross, where we may find forgiveness, new joy, new peace.

"Come." It is the most beautiful word in the English language. Hospitality, friendship, tenderness, love, pity, confidence—all are expressed in this word. The spirit of this word is rapidly becoming alien to our generation so ruled by hate and suspicion and selfishness. It is the only spirit which can heal our wounded souls.

"Come." This invitation is for you. Come to the cross where we are one—sinners reclaimed. Come to God; come *back* to God, who has made you and redeemed you.

Chapter Nine

C*ome* for personal cleansing

Text: Isaiah 1:18; I John 1:7b

"Come now, and let us reason together, saith the Lord: though your sins be as scarlet, they shall be as white as snow; though they be red like crimson, they shall be as wool." . . . "The blood of Jesus Christ his Son cleanseth us from all sin."

IT IS often dangerous to repeat well-known truths. It is dangerous because of our human love for systematizing and organizing. In the systematizing, power becomes pattern, and the truth may lose its force. In the organizing, spirit becomes form, and the truth may lose its edge. This has happened periodically with Christian truth, so that men, offered a system of thought and pious platitudes in lieu of the truth, grow weary and cry out for something new.

The invitation, "Come for personal cleansing," has been heard so much that persons often mistake the ability to recite it or to understand the theology of the phrase for the deeper personal meaning. When this deeper meaning is lost, Communism can justifiably say that Christianity with its teaching of forgiveness is an opiate for the people; and cynics can justifiably scoff at the converts to Christ found on Pacific Isles, who were fully as *dishonest* as the heathen because they used the doctrine of that forgiveness to cover everything!

But, dangerous or not, this invitation must be repeated, and repeated at every possible opportunity. The invitation of God to come for personal cleansing remains the heart of the Christian message. Even the non-Christian sees this, for, as a Buddhist priest appropriately said, when asked the difference between his own faith and Christianity, "Christianity offers the forgiveness of sins." The message of the cross, backed by the promises of God, is simply, "Come, sinner, and receive forgiveness." Without this, we have no message.

We shall not spend much time in either proving or defining sin. Why should we? The whole realm of human experience underscores at every step its grim reality. From the time a child, scolded by its mother, hangs its head in an intuitive acknowledgment of wrong, until he lies on his deathbed, fearing the future because behind him he can remember little but wrongdoing, he finds sin the plainest fact of human existence. Our only trouble with the fact of sin is that we dislike so much to face it.

For one thing, we have come to prize some-thing we term our individuality, our distinctive-ness. We have built a code of individualism which excuses anything so long as it makes us different and sets us apart. People laugh at our quirks and speak admiringly of our individuality, and this is much easier to hear than that this individuality is simply an over-inflated ego, or subtle selfish-ness, or simple lust. Sin, then, becomes so in-grown, so woven into the very fabric of our per-sonalities, that to face it may involve a major operation; and we fear, quite rightly, that should we submit, there will be little of the true self left. For instance, what is there to Tommy Manville if you remove his eight (or is it nine?) wives? What would be left of most of us if our sensitivity (which is usually an over-exposed ego), or our indulgence (which is usually a form of selfish-ness) were taken out? We have built the structure of our personalities squarely around our sins.

We think we have done it because it insures our being different. "A man must be himself," we say. But the real reason is that it is the best possible way of hiding the sin. When we make our sins into personality traits, the sin itself be-comes less conspicuous.

Then, too, there is fear. We are afraid that if this sin should be removed, life would become frightfully uneventful. Try to convince a drunk-ard that life could be happy without his liquor, regardless of how much he might profess to wish to be cured of his habit. Try to convince an adulterer that life could be happy without his lust, even though he might profess to pine for a happy home and one mate. Try to convince the skeptic that life could be happy without his doubts, even if he does say, "I'd like to believe what you believe." Our lives are built about our sins, and the prospect of life without them looks too bleak. Try to tell the crowd-minded that life could be just as full, and much more valuable, without his cronies, even though he realizes their degrading influence. Men just don't believe it!

No, we don't need to *prove* the fact of sin. Its inescapable reality meets us wherever we turn. We need the insight to detect it, and the integrity to admit it. The man who faces sin, who quits running from conscience, is in a quandary. God has overtaken him, and he is quite disconcerted! In the words of the poet:

"I sat alone with my conscience
   In a place where time had ceased,
   And we talked of my former living
   In the land where the years increased;
   And I felt I should have to answer
   The question as put to me,
   And to face the question and answer
   Throughout eternity.
   The ghosts of forgotten actions

Came floating before my sight,
And things that I thought were dead things,
Were alive with a terrible might."

Sin needs no proving, but it does need to be
met and solved. The longer we live, the more do
we realize that life here takes on a singular aspect:
"I must deal with my sin." As Paul stated it, we
must "work out our salvation in fear and trembling." This is the crucial fact.

When the sinner realizes he is a sinner, he can
say but two things: "Oh, what have I done; what
have I done?" And then, "What can I do; what
can I do?"

Into the void in the heart of the repentant sinner there comes the haunting invitation of God:
"Come . . . though your sins be as scarlet, they
shall be as snow; though they be red like crimson, they shall be as wool." And the testimony of
a cleansed John: "The blood of Jesus Christ
cleanseth us from all sin."

At this point, the sinner makes a correct obser-
vation: "This is wonderful news, but how can it
be possible? I am too sin-sick." Sin-consciousness
always produces a sense of indebtedness and a feeling of helplessness. A taut desperation takes possession of the heart. God has been found, but He
is so far away. And yet He is so desperately needed. He hovers over the horizon of the sin-conscious
one, taunting him, it seems, with visions of the

only life, unattainable now because of his sins.
It wasn't always this way, though. There was a
time when He was quite near, perhaps on the day
of confirmation, or that day he promised so fervently to serve Him, that day he sang with youth-
ful voice, "Living for Jesus a life that is true."
Somehow, the specter of sin was something taught
in a book then, or limited to other terrible people. But now, like cancer, it has struck home.
Wherever he turns, he sees sin. It looms larger
and larger. The worst part of it is, it is unexplainable. Those little pranks didn't seem so bad at
the time. But even more than that, he didn't realize that he was what he now finds himself to be—
sin-sick, sin-saturated. It isn't that he is doing
anything worse than he did last year. Not that.
It is simply that God is not so near now, because
this sin which he sees in himself is such an insurmountable obstacle.

And the refrain re-echoes, "What can I do?"
Some join the church, or go into social work, or
even become missionaries and ministers. They
think perhaps such action will help. But this sin
is too far-reaching to be alleviated by such a surface gesture, however sincerely it may be made.
It is something deep, stemming from inside. It
cannot be undone. It cannot be compensated for.

"Come, let us reason together." "Come." That
word again! Shall the sinner never be rid of it?
No, not so long as there is a cross in the center

of that "Come," and a blood-stained Savior. He
shall never escape it. This sin must be overcome.
Cleanness must take the place of sin. God says,
"Come—for personal cleansing. Be washed of
your sin. Be made completely clean, whole, refreshed. Simply come to me."

In the words of the poet,

"Come, ye sinners, poor and needy;
  Weak and wounded, sick and sore;
  Jesus ready stands to save you,
  Full of pity, love, and power.
  He is able; He is willing; doubt no more."

Then the reserve breaks down. Perhaps in an
unguarded moment, or in a moment of deliberate choice—it makes no difference how—he tells
Him everything, of his resentments about Him,
his quarrels with others, and, above all, this great
problem of sin. And that is all there is to it. Sin
is defeated, forgiveness has conquered, despair
gives way to peace. Such a God as we have! "Come
—I receive sinners."

It is quite possible that none of you have
ever been brought to this emotional pitch, but it
is probable that most of you have at some time
or other been engaged in a battle with this sin of
yours. Then consider. Is there anything else that
you have found in life which can win the battle
against sin? Can *you*, in your own self-made good-

ness and self-set moral standards? Can your friends, or your church, even? The world struggles endlessly with this problem of sin; and also you and I, until we come to that place where we stand and say, in our own way, "The cross has the answer. It alone can cancel the debt of my sin. It alone can absolve me before the judgment seat of God. It alone can restore peace within me, and restore my sonship with God." If sin is to be dealt with, God must do it. I am tainted with it, and so is everyone else. God must handle it. The Word says He did it through Jesus, whose blood on the cross cleanses me.

Whether we are driven by emotion or by logic, it is you and I who actually make the decision. We simply will to believe and to accept the fact of forgiveness of sin through Jesus on the cross. And God, through His Holy Spirit, does the work.

So the hymn-writer had a keen insight when he wrote, "Nothing in my hands I bring—simply to Thy cross I cling." God calls us for personal cleansing, and cleanses us by absorbing in Himself our guilt.

"Just as I am, and waiting not
To rid my soul of one dark blot,
To Thee, whose blood can cleanse each spot,
O Lamb of God, I come, I come."

Chapter Ten

Come to satisfy spiritual hunger

Text: Isaiah 55:1; John 7:37

"Ho, every one that thirsteth, come ye to
the waters, and he that hath no money;
come ye, buy, and eat; yea, come, buy
wine and milk without money and without price." . . . "In that great day of the
feast, Jesus stood and cried, saying, If any
man thirst, let him come unto me, and
drink."

THE Norwegian writer, Garborg, has coined
a phrase which is strikingly apt in its description of many moderns. He calls them "tired old
men." He is not referring to those who have
spent a normal lifetime in hard labor and are
now drawing to the natural close of a worthy life.
He is referring to young men, middle-aged men
and women, who should be throbbing with life's
full vigor, and yet are in spirit and in outlook
"tired old men."

Something has happened to make people like
that. You have seen them, haven't you? Perhaps

you are one of them. They are the ones who are
entirely bored with life, meeting life's great op-
portunities with a barely stifled yawn. They are
bent in spirit, and bent in body, as they carry
around with them a load of useless cares. They
face the future with dulled eyes, never even seeing the horizon.

What has happened to these men and women?
Something has been draining their strength. That
is obvious. The prophet Isaiah has an answer.
He says that they have been eating food which
perishes, so that life for them has become a cease-
less round of intense work to get more food
which instantly perishes, so that they must work
some more for more of the same, ad infinitum.
Lin Yutang, the Chinese author, in his book,
Through Tears and Laughter, says his teachers
taught him that the white man was forced to go
through life carrying a heavy burden on his back,
and he had always wondered what it was. Then
he found out. The white man was wearing himself out carrying a sack of "canned goods"! There
is more truth than humor in that.

We have eaten and drunk of something called
"liberty," but it has turned out to be license. We
have partaken of something which was called
"new thought," but it has turned out to be "no
thought." We have developed something called
"broad-mindedness," and now we don't know
what we think. We have concocted cups of plea-

sure, and they have turned out to be bitter dregs. We sample of the arts, taste of philosophy, sniff at a bit of economics, hear the names of some great men (and call it history), cram in some "best-sellers" (and become well-read), listen with a worried look to the news commentators, scan the newspaper headlines, indulge in some street-corner gossip (and become authorities on world affairs), and then add a bit of foul humor for spice. This hodgepodge, we say, will produce a well-rounded person.

This is the stuff we are feeding upon. Small wonder we are "tired old men"! Small wonder that we are distracted, nervous, bored! Small wonder that we cannot cope with new situations without a book of directions! Small wonder that we are empty, hollow, in that place we call our soul, when our soul should be filled with richness! We have been feeding our spirits upon trash—and wonder why we are not satisfied.

Our problem is simply that we are spiritually hungry, undernourished. There is an alarming apathy of the spirit among even the best of us. So we dope ourselves with sensationalism, dupe ourselves by listening to the best preachers, and do nothing more

Listen to such a person as Walter Lippmann, in his *Preface to Morals,* sum up the results. Looking for spiritual satisfaction he found instead: "The evidences" (of spiritual malnutrition) "lie all about us: in the brave and brilliant atheists who have defied the fundamentalist God, and have become very nervous; in the women who have emancipated themselves from the tyranny of fathers, husbands, and homes, and with the intermittent and expensive help of a psychoanalyst, are now enduring liberty as interior decorators; in the young man and woman who is world-weary at twenty-two; in the multitudes who drug themselves with pleasure; in the crowds enfranchised by the blood of heroes who cannot be persuaded to take an interest in their destiny; in the millions at last free to think without fear of preacher or policeman, who have made the moving picture and the popular newspapers what they are."

Spiritual emptiness is a terrible thing. We try to find a standard of comparison, so we compare it to the pangs of starvation; to wandering, delirious, in a desert without food or water; and still we cannot adequately picture it.

Listen, then, to Renan, the Frenchman, who tried to find spiritual satisfaction apart from the Church, and admitted: "The enchanted circle which embraces the whole of life is broken, and there is a feeling of emptiness like that which follows an attack of fever or an unhappy love affair." Listen to Nietzsche, the German philosopher, who, after a lifetime of feeding his soul upon thoughts of man's greatness, had only this to say:

"Where is my home? For it do I ask and seek, and have sought, but have not found it. O eternal everywhere, O eternal nowhere, O eternal in vain!"

Most of us are not so tempestuous, so poetic, about our discontent with life. Perhaps we have less sensitive spirits and fail to see so clearly just how we are deluding ourselves. We simply express it by quarrels at meal-time, by slamming the door in vexation, or by an occasional outburst of profanity. It is possible to live, as so many are doing, feeding the soul on "old wives' tales," thoughts about the weather, worry about the stomach, flurries of entertainment, eating, sleeping, and drinking, and to get along with only an occasional headache as a result, just a touch of nervousness, a bit of confusion, a hint of anxiety. It is possible to be an average citizen, and pass a casual examination, and be termed absolutely "normal." But this is not life, either in God's sense, or our own. There remains that emptiness, that hunger.

No, there is something deeper in man's soul, something which is not satisfied by feeding upon commonplaces. Instinctively, we all recognize this need. It is a hunger and a thirst for something deeper than etiquette, nobler than idealism, more satisfying than friendship. It is a hunger for something of eternal consequence. But suppose we were equipped only with this longing, this intuitive realization that we need God, that life on a purely human level is not enough? How frustrated we would be!

God has not left us, however, with nothing more than a dream of Him. He has moved to satisfy our hunger, by moving in, Himself, into our void. We call it "revelation." That is, He has told us about Himself, introduced Himself to us. And, thanks be, He has not stopped there. He has not set Himself up as a puzzle, a riddle for us to ponder, as something we give to our children to keep them occupied when they are discontented. He has done more than that.

He has offered Himself to us for our *use*. Everything that is God Himself He has extended to us. That is the meaning of the invitation of Jesus: "Come unto me, ye who are thirsty," and again when He said: "My flesh is food indeed, and my blood is drink indeed," and again, "I shall be, in that man who comes, a well of living water, springing up into eternal life." That is what Isaiah meant when he invited us: "Ho, everyone that thirsteth—come." That is what David meant when he said with deep contentment, "My heart is inditing a good matter: I think of the things pertaining to the Lord."

In the face of such an invitation, how long shall we continue our foolish disregard for spiritual truth? Don't make the mistake many do, of thinking that if you just add a bit of "religion" to your spiritual diet you have found the answer. It may help, of course, to determinedly mumble a prayer at noon each day and think about God at three o'clock in the afternoon. But that is not what is meant by coming to Him to satisfy spiritual hunger.

We are really to feed upon Him. This means that we begin our days with prayer, asking for guidance, for strength. This means that we live our days around His Word—family devotions, if you please. This means that the church service becomes the fountain-head for an entire week of living. This means that we approach God *expecting* to be filled. This means that the cross becomes more than a nice ornament and attractive altar dressing; it becomes the point at which we rally all our energy, and from which we derive all our spiritual satisfactions

This can't be done merely by making a resolution. That old lady whose face lights up so when she is reading the Word, who is so thrilled with a visit from the pastor, who says when given private communion, "I was so hungry for my Lord," didn't become like that over night. Such an attitude is the culmination of a life-time lived in actual dependence upon God. Such people have, all their lives, taken all their worries to Him; all their fears, all their sins. They have, all their lives, been content with following the thoughts of God and feeding themselves upon those thoughts. And now, in the crucial period of old age and impending death, they are not afraid. They are strong in a strength outside themselves. They have been nourished by Him.

To feed upon God, then, is to be content with His word for your life. This contentment comes when you have entrusted yourself to Him, to His will for your life. To feed upon God is to seek His presence through the pages of Scripture. To feed upon God is to spend our days "beneath the cross of Jesus," where He gave Himself to us in the body and blood of His Son. To feed upon God is to live in communion with the living Christ. Then can we sing too, "My cup runneth over."

We are all hungry for God. We seem to be born with that hunger, and until we find Him we are undernourished. Substitutes may deceive for a time, but they do not satisfy. It is God for whom we were born, and Him we must have.

God has offered Himself to us in the form of a crucified Christ, promising that if we come to Him, feed upon Him, let Him enrich our lives, our lives will be full. We have the promise of God that He is sufficient, and the testimony of those who have come and found Him to be so.

Come—to satisfy spiritual hunger.

Chapter Eleven

Come to a safe place

Text: Genesis 7:1

"And the Lord said unto Noah, Come thou
and all thy house into the ark."

A RUBBER life raft was picked up by a U. S.
Navy cruiser. Its passengers, who had been
adrift for many days without adequate food or
water or protection from the sun, were taken
aboard. They were near exhaustion from the ordeal. Once they were safely on board ship, they
were asked what it was they wanted most. Food?
Drink? Rest? They answered, "Thank you; after
a while. Just now we'd like to sit and do nothing
else than to realize we are secure and safe."

"Just to realize we are secure"—there is the secret yearning of every mortal man. We are creatures of fear and worry. We fear poverty, so we
invest in our insurance and pension plans, our
stocks and bonds and real estate, and we vote for
the man who promises us the most at the least
cost. We fear sickness, so we scurry to our clinics,
to our health clubs, our once-a-year bodily check-

ups, eat our pills, and clutter the operating table. We fear loneliness, so we hang on grimly to our families, and to numbers, even if it means merely clinging to the skirts of a large city. We fear neurosis (the bug-a-boo word of our generation), and flock to the psychologists, and read books on mental health. We fear bombs, so we build our armies and our United Nations. We fear death, so we do everything in our power to prevent it, and failing in this, we join organizations which profess to give a sure answer to its mystery.

Life does need a certain amount of temporal security to stand the strain of living. But it is a fact that, given food, home, friends, good health, fine armies, good government, and everything else pertaining to our temporal needs, we are still afraid. We still worry. We still wake up and live anxiously. We might lose our money, or our health, we reason with ourselves. Then what?

Intuitively we recognize a need for a more basic security, a deeper, farther-reaching assurance than these can provide. Perhaps we have become so busy searching and working for security that the search has become an end in itself. Perhaps our efforts toward security have become so intense that we have lost sight of our true goal. Or still worse, we have given ourselves to a material security which defeats itself and which eventually not only fails to make secure but actually makes us more fearful.

A man was dreaming about a model house. As he dreamed, he built. This was to be the perfect house, one which could never be improved upon. Before he knew what had happened, he had almost finished the building. He stepped back to survey it, to admire his handiwork. It was indeed beautiful. He stepped in to see it from the inside, and soon noticed that with each step the walls trembled a little. It was beautiful, but insecure, because he had forgotten to put in the braces where they should be put, and the right thickness in the supporting walls. He had built a beautiful house, but his house had become his worry.

Something like that has happened to us. We have laid our plans and built upon them an intricate, amazing building of physical comforts, economic protection, and all the rest—and we are afraid to live in it. It might collapse. The supports haven't been put in the right places, and the undergirding has been omitted entirely. Whatever stuff we build our Towers of Babel of, they will eventually collapse.

There is in us all a longing for the assurance that "underneath are the everlasting arms," that somewhere there is a foundation on which we can build securely a life which will last. Our search is for a security of the spirit, where "rust does not consume, and thieves do not break through and steal." Our need is a security of the inner man, something of the type that Job found, a sense of belonging which can withstand both loss and worry. Our quest is for a God who is more than an abstraction, or a theory, or a formula; for a God who is a Person, and the type of Person to whom we can turn when fear overtakes us.

In this much we are correct. Our trouble lies in the fact that we are so anxious for security that we fail to see that it is not found without a certain risk, a definite gamble. We must dare to believe, with Noah, that the Ark which God has prepared is adequate. I have no doubt that the Ark seemed rather insufficient in the face of the fury of the coming storm, but Noah took the chance, followed God's invitation, and found security.

The cross gathers into focal point and solves all our foolish fears: our fear of men, our fear of force, our fear of defeat, our fear of physical and economic loss, our fear of death. On the cross they were all met, and surmounted by our Lord. God invites us to believe this and to test our belief by coming to Him.

Listen to the testimony of those who have believed and accepted this invitation. The Psalmist sings, "God is our refuge and strength," and again, "In the day of trouble . . . He will lift me up upon a rock." Paul testifies, "All things work together for good to them that love God." There must be something to it. And Jesus Himself said, "Fear not them who kill the body, but cannot kill the soul," and again, "Why take ye thought for tomorrow? Your heavenly Father will care for you." It runs all through the Word, this insistence that we are meant to find our refuge on His breast. Nothing of value can vanish from a life entrusted to His care.

One of our problems lies in the fact that we are ashamed of our fears. We apologize for our weaknesses, and try to cover up our anxieties. We realize that we ought to be bigger than we are, so we practice a bit of Stoicism in the hope that nobody will notice. We resolve to worry in silence, alone. But the minute we do this, we have really missed the true nature of God Himself. Life at times does become more than we can endure. When God said, "Be thou faithful unto death," it was not a command which we must fulfill alone. It was an invitation to try Him out. Fatigue *can* work great havoc with the nervous system, and a sudden shock *can* undermine many years of work. Illness *does* test our faith, as do sorrow and bereavement. The loss of possessions *is* a cause for concern. Why, then, are we ashamed to admit that these things bother us? Is it not because deep within us, in our heart of hearts, we realize that we do not have the faith to overcome these worries and sorrows?

But, then, what is faith? Is it merely a Stoicism with a Christian terminology? Or is it dependence? It is dependence. Then, why should we not venture out in it and find out what it can do? It is noteworthy that most of those pictured in the New Testament came to Christ and found God in Him because their worries drove them to Him.

That is precisely what God's invitation means. When our worries and fears loom large, we are to permit God to do for us what He has pledged Himself to do. We are to permit Him to be our safe place in the storm, our security. How is this done?

It is done in the same way that a child finds refuge in its father's arms—by running into them. The problem child is one who is not content with the natural way of things, a child who will not permit its parent to be its refuge. For a little child, by nature, can do only one thing—permit itself to be loved, fed, washed, clothed, cared for. As the child withdraws, it is removed from comfort and security. Likewise, our great privilege as God's children is simply to permit Him to be our shield and refuge.

A man, seemingly healthy and vigorous, young and energetic, equipped with a radiant faith, was stricken one day with a fit of worry. The worry concerned his health, and grew to such proportions that it became a question in his mind whether he would live through each of the succeeding twenty-four hours. Doctors called it fatigue, with nothing organically wrong. The man was in despair. He couldn't live with himself. He hated to admit it might be a nervous breakdown. He hardly knew what to pray about, but he prayed. Prayer, however, seemed to help little. He cast about everywhere to find help. There seemed to be none available. So he prayed, incessantly, wherever he was, whatever he was doing. Little happened, except that he was driven into the Word and into constant prayer. One day he realized, to his amazement, that when he was in prayer his load seemed lighter. He knew he had found the answer. The healing process was slow, but sure. It entailed nothing more than heeding God's invitation, by bringing to Him every fear which plagued the mind, every resentment, every doubt, yes, every sin, and saying, "I leave this with You." Then peace came. Not miraculously, and certainly not overnight, mind you. But it came. It came because he had been forced to heed God's tender invitation, "Come."

Now this acceptance had its price. He had to let go of himself, and all the other props which had seemingly been his security. He had to let them go, because while he clung to them, he could not reach God. As he let go, there came that calm certainty that God is, and that God cares, which is the essence of "the peace that passes all understanding."

Fears do not come to such a head in every life. Most persons are equipped with a nervous strength to keep them in check. But they are there, plaguing every life. They are evident in

so many ways, and they must be met. They can
only be met as God is permitted to bear them.
They are only met as God becomes the One in
whom we "live and move, and have our being."

"Come." Thank God for your misfortunes,
your worries. Thank God for them! They may be
the very agency which can drive you to find Him
in Jesus Christ, without whom life is unlivable.

> "Beneath the cross of Jesus
> I fain would take my stand,
> The shadow of a mighty rock
> Within a weary land;
> A home within the wilderness . . . "

But, many of those who come to the cross are
finding no peace. Instead of a refuge, they find
they are on more stormy waters than ever. God
has become, not a restorer of peace but the tor-
mentor of their consciences. What is the trouble?

They have come by paths of their own choosing, disdaining the path which God has opened
for them. In an illustrated edition of Bunyan's
Pilgrim's Progress there is a picture which shows
Christian standing inside the Walled City. He
is noticing two men who are jumping over the
walls in their eagerness to enter the security
of the city. He reprimands them for not going
through the gate, and assures them that there is
security only for those who go through that gate.

God has prepared the way. The way is the

cross of Jesus Christ. Many are they who endeavor to leap over the walls, seeking refuge without having to bear the shame of the cross. But the cross is inescapably before us if we seek in God security. There is no other way. Paul came this way, and his song of jubilee is re-echoed by all who follow: "If God be for us, who can be against us? For I am persuaded that neither death, nor life, nor angels, nor principalities, nor powers, nor things present, nor things to come, nor height, nor depth, nor any other creature, shall be able to separate us from the love of God, *which is in Christ Jesus our Lord.*"

Chapter Twelve

Come to good fellowship

Numbers 10:29; Matthew 18:20

"And Moses said unto Hobab, . . . We are journeying unto the place of which the Lord said, I will give it you: Come thou with us and we will do thee good." . . . "Where two or three are gathered together in my name, there am I in the midst of them."

COME—we will do thee good." Moses extended this invitation to his brother-in-law when the Israelites were preparing to resume their journey to the promised land. It is really an audacious invitation. Moses asserts that the fellowship in the camp of the Israelites will be more beneficial to Hobab, despite its rigors, than the comforts of home.

This is an allegory of the relation of the Christian church to the world. Since we, as Christians, are engaged constantly in the sad business of breaking camp, and leaving the security of the home base for the pilgrimage, it is our constant responsibility to say to our friends, too, "Come with us. Leave this way of life. Enter our fellowship. We will do you good." But do we have that confidence in our Christian fellowship? Can you say to your relative that if he will walk with you through life you can help him?

Is it not true that such boldness seems a part of our Christian history, rather than the stamp of our present-day Christianity? Often we convey the impression that we are not at all sure that our fellowship is worth while. We issue our invitations so often with an apology, a defense. We are so hesitant, so reasonable, so polite, that our invitation does not ring true. We have given homage to a distorted image called "tolerance" for so long that the goddess has robbed us of our confidence in our cause. Yet the need of the world is, as Karl Barth reminds us, for "someone to speak the word of certainty with certainty."

Our weak condition was strikingly revealed in a seminar class in a post-graduate theological school. The class was invited to suggest questions suitable for discussion. A missionary, home on furlough, ventured this question: "Do we, on the mission fields, have the right to proselyte among those who study in our schools? That is, have we the right to try to convert them to our Christian faith?" And he was in earnest, this missionary, whose very title implies that he is out

in the world for but one purpose, namely, to say,
"Come with us—we will do you good!" The teacher, with ponderous thoughtfulness, replied, "That
is a good question." Yes, indeed, a good question! For both teacher and pupil thereby testify
to the bankruptcy of their faith. They are not
sure it is worth selling!

This text provides a good occasion to pause for
a serious re-examination of our Christian fellowship. Do we still believe in ourselves? Have we
kept this Moses audacity? Are we acquainted with
the spirit of Paul, who, as he stood before King
Felix on trial for his life, could not refrain from
giving the invitation even to the King in the
words, "I wish you could be as I am, free in
Christ, yet without these bonds"? Do we in our
congregation have such a spirit? Is there such a
contagion in our Christian fellowship, radiating
into our community?

Let us investigate. Many of you have extended
an invitation for your church. Fine. How did
you do it? To what did your invitation testify? I
venture a guess. I venture that the primary purpose of the church, the first quality of healthy
Christian fellowship, ran a poor second to the
music in the service, the personality of the pastor,
the games at Young People's, the food at Ladies'
Aid. Now, there is nothing really wrong with
such invitations. They may be true, they may be
made in good faith, and they may even be given

with the secret hope of luring our friends into a deeper Christian understanding, by using this back door. But such an approach is at best misleading. It directs the attention to these secondary things. It implies that you have found these secondary values to be of the most importance. We are too preoccupied in our every-day living with this dabbling around in the peripheral things, and attempting to make them appear vital, as it is. The church is concerned with issues far too great, and is playing for too great stakes, to be taken up with these imitations. We have no right to substitute for the genuine fellowship we have with one another as Christians, in Christ, anything less than that. If the friend who is thus approached is really discerning, he will say, "No thank you. I have enough of such things now."

When we Christians say "Come," it must be to a peculiar fellowship, to something totally different from that of the average club, something transcending that of family relationships and cliques. We must dare to believe that we possess a spiritual insight and a spiritual strength which the world as such does not know. We must be conscious of a spiritual vitality which makes us convincing when we say, "Come with us— you need us."

There must be a daring about our invitation, as there was with Moses. Not cocksureness, not

arrogance, not superiority—but the sort of daring which is born from an experience which cannot be doubted, and makes of our invitation a
challenge. Moses could say this because he had
had an experience. The church can say this only
on the strength of a deep-seated experience. We
must have the experience of having heard and
heeded this invitation of God, of having tried it
in the test-tubes of daily living. Only when we
can speak from experience can we be either inviting or convincing.

A romantic chapter of modern life is being
enacted by the organization Alcoholics Anon-
ymous. Its members are a picture of what our true
role in life should be. They are cured alcoholics,
who have banded themselves together for the
purpose of helping to cure other victims. In their
eagerness to serve, they place themselves on 24-
hour call, ready to go to the help of a fellow-man
in need. When they invite others to their testimony meetings, they actually say, "Come with us
—we can help you"—and folks believe them!

The Christian church, then, should be a clinic,
with her doors wide open. Over the doors should
be inscribed, "Come with us—we will do you
good." As the sick, the down-trodden, the poor,
the untouchables, the unlikeables, the worried,
the sin-laden come through the doors, we should
be able to greet them with a loving spirit, a
knowledge of their diseases, and an acquaintance-

ship with the cure. There must be strength in us. We must be able to point to the Great Physician. As we sit down with them and hear their complaints, it must be in the spirit of, "Yes, I know how it is. I was once like that, but I have met Jesus Christ. He can help you, too." *And we must be able to lead these folks to Jesus.*

Is this the picture of our Christian fellowship? Or have we become like the chameleon, reflecting only the spirit of the community in which we happen to be located, welcoming into our select group only those of our social standing, our tastes, our incomes? The Christian church, which is intended to be the one place where the "banker, the baker, the candlestick-maker" can sit down together in the same pew, as one, has in too many cases forfeited this birthright. To reclaim this birthright involves an experience which alone makes men one. What is this experience?

We must experience the sinfulness of our sin. Otherwise the confidence we exhibit will be merely self-righteousness, and a spiritual arrogance. These attributes have frightened away many more than they have attracted. Such an experience transformed self-righteous Saul into Paul, the missionary. Whenever he spoke, men listened, because they could sense that he was thinking of himself as the "chief of sinners." Has the *fact* of sin become meaningful to you in terms of *your* sin?

We must experience the validity and the power of the Word of God. The distress of our day is in large part due to the fact that we have lost our respect for the "Thus saith the Lord" which motivated the prophets and caused even the rebellious sinners to hear them with trembling. When God becomes real and personal for us, through His Word, He breathes some of His majesty into our souls. Much truth is in the expression, "Our fathers feared God, and nothing else; we have been emancipated from our fear of God, and are afraid of everything else." Peter demonstrates what happens when we live in an obedient relationship to His Word. When the rulers of the synagogue sought to have him refrain from preaching, he was able to reply, "We ought to obey God rather than men." And, because God's Word was so real in that situation, this same Peter was able to make such a beautiful gift to the crippled beggar on the temple steps: "What I have I give thee, in the name of Jesus Christ, arise." Is God's Word operative in your life?

We must experience the gracious meaning of Jesus Christ as the answer to sin and the interpretation of that Word. The invitation was stated for us one time by a lady of Samaria who had met Jesus by the well, and who ran back to her fellow townsmen, saying excitedly, "Come, meet a man who has told me all that I have ever done." A wave of revival followed that invitation. It was expressed by one called Nathanael, who ran to Peter and said, "Come, I have met the Christ." A great soul was won by that invitation. But you see, they had had an experience of Jesus! And really, have we any business even intruding into the affairs of others, unless we can speak with the same authenticity? If we cannot, we make of the church merely a great debating society. But we were called to be witnesses, not lawyers. When we speak from experience, men listen with the respect we give to anybody who gives the impression of knowing what he is talking about.

At this point we must be wary. It is possible to make the *form* of the experience of first importance, and to grow impatient with an experience which does not match ours. When this happens, we breed bigotry, and point subtly to ourselves and *our* experience, rather than to the Christ whom we have met, who *is* our experience, and who has placed His stamp upon the substance of our fellowship when He said, "Where two or three are gathered together in my name, there am I in the midst of them." It is the universality of the experience which is its strength. It is not limited to types of personalities, nor to types of problems. The form of the experience is merely the avenue by which we meet Him.

Before Him the intellectual doubter finds his questions answered; the guilt-conscious one is given peace; the seeker after truth and beauty is satisfied; the earnest thinker is enlightened. Each will say the same, "Come with us, we can help you," because Christ has actually helped each one, in his way. In each there will be the temptation to assume that his is the only valid experience—and it is—for him! Yet, even so, there is a kinship in this fellowship, which is explained by the validity of each experience, and the all-embracing greatness of the Christ. When such folks meet and converse on the things of the spirit, they really speak in tongues, for they employ the common language of men who have met the Savior. Together they say, "Come with us—we can help you." They can say it, because they know best of all that their strength does not lie in themselves.

It is inherent in the life of Christianity that each generation rediscover this truth for itself. Until we do, we have no message to bring to our troubled world. Until we do, we have no invitation to give; we can only add to the confusion by adding our opinions to the countless others. Christ must meet our fellow-men, through us. We must keep Him living in our community by the regular assembling of ourselves together as Christians.

The world owes its life to this Christian communion. The Greek word for church, "ekklesia," means "that which is called out." The church, then, is the fellowship of redeemed men, men who have been called out from the comforts of home and have joined the pilgrimage. As these men travel, they are busy with one work, to call others into their fellowship. Even as the cities of Sodom and Gomorrah owed their second chance to the loving concern of Abraham, for whom God was willing to spare those wicked cities, if only ten righteous could be found in them—so does the world owe its existence to the church in its midst, which is prayerfully busy night and day reclaiming the souls of the lost. In this sense, even your community is indebted to the fellowship of the faithful which it contains.

Perhaps some member of this Christian fellowship has been inviting you, "Come with us—we will do you good." Do not shun or avoid him. Above all, do not fear him. He seeks your true welfare. He is the voice of God, calling you, and who knows whether God will ever speak to you in any other way?

Above all, let each one ask himself, in the words of the hymn-writer:

> "My Jesus, am I in that band,
> And wilt Thou call me Thine?
> Do I among the chosen stand
> Whose lamps so brightly shine?"

Chapter Thirteen

Come for rest of soul

Text: Matthew 11:28; Colossians 1:20

> "Come unto me, all ye that labour and are
> heavy laden, and I will give you rest." . . .
> "And having made peace through the blood
> of his cross, by him to reconcile all
> things unto himself."

THIS beautiful text tells us that God's father-
ly goodness is the one completely dependable
factor in life. It tells us that when we suspect life
of being heartless and cold, in the very center of
things there throbs the heart of a loving Father.
It doesn't prove God to us; it simply shows us
what He is. I wonder whether the poet Whittier
had been reading this text when he wrote, "I only
know I cannot drift beyond His love and care."

The spectacle of Jesus standing in the midst
of our tired world and saying, "Come unto me
all ye who labor and are heavy laden, and I will
give you rest," is the most elusive aspect of the
Gospel. Yet this truth must be grasped if we are
to be helped by Jesus Christ.

If we are to grasp it, we must begin by ridding

our minds of some common misconceptions
about God. We must be rid of the assumption
that we must become "good Christians" before
this invitation is for us. We must quit thinking
that God is an overly-strict parent who rewards
and comforts us only when we have behaved ourselves. We must see Him exactly as He has revealed Himself in this text—a Father whose heart
is aching to help us *regardless of our moral or
spiritual condition.* Jesus did not make this offer
to His disciples alone. He did not make it to the
Pharisees and the Priests. He did not leave any
strings attached to it. We do not need to understand the law in order to be able to respond to
this invitation. We do not need to go through
some process whereby the law shall pin us down
and convince us of our sinfulness in order to accept this invitation.

All we need in order to respond is to be tired, to
be worried, to be tense, to be puzzled. All we need
is to be all worn out by our daily work, by the
sickness of our child or mate or parent, all tied
up in knots over the prospect of providing daily
food for our families in the face of rising costs and
fixed salaries. All we need is to be weighted down
by the cares of this life. It is so difficult for the
human understanding to grasp this. Yet all of
Jesus' revelations throb with this undiscriminat-
ing, loving outreach. "Whosoever cometh to me,
I will in no wise cast out," are His words. "God so

loved the world . . . that *whosoever* believeth on Him shall not perish," writes John. We know that this applies to the heathen and that therefore we must send our missionaries. But do we understand that in our own home town, yes, in our very congregation, these words apply with exactly the same meaning? "Come—*all.*" Regardless of who you are, or what you are, or where you are, come. Regardless of whether you have come to church regularly or not, or whether you have contributed or not; regardless, even, of whether you love, hate, or are indifferent to this Jesus—this invitation is for you.

Here Jesus offers Himself as the rallying point for our problems, and especially for our soul-weariness. Certainly we need a new rallying point. All the other means by which we have tried to revive ourselves have successively failed—pleasure, cynicism, thought, drugs—all have failed, and leave us more weary than before. Deep within the soul-weariness of our world is a wistful longing for something more solid. There is an awareness of a need for God. In the words of Augustine, "Our hearts are restless until they rest in Thee."

What is causing this weariness? We have ready answers. We work too hard, we say; but even as we say it, we realize that our problem lies deeper than that. It is the tension, the inner strain and conflict of living in this world. Contemporary man is a boiling pot of wishes and desires that are at war with one another and with those of his fellows. As Professor Sorokin says, "Our whole system of culture is a house divided against itself. It suffers from a tragic and fatal dualism of glorifying man and degrading him at the same time." We want what we should not have, because it is not good for us, or it belongs to our neighbor. Our family life both satisfies and wears us out. Our friends both annoy and entertain us. Our high-pressure age is causing us to work against time and schedule. As one man put it, "Life today compels us to work up a full head of steam, but we have to keep it within ourselves, and it just churns around inside, wearing us out." Maybe a good nap would help, but we arise with the same tautness. If we could understand, just for a moment, the Hindu teaching of self-suspension!

One way of dealing with these tensions is to say as some ladies do, "If anything else happens, I'll scream!" But this hardly satisfies, and only irritates the listener. Or we can deal with these tensions as certain psychologists tell us to, by simply "expressing ourselves." But doing just what we want to do, when we want to do it, doesn't usually work. We want to do so badly what we shouldn't! We need a deeper relaxing point. Jesus invites us to relax in Him, and promises us—not release, not temporary help, but something far deeper. He promises us rest, peace, a sense of well-being.

He invites us, first, to a Person, Jesus Christ.
We are restless, not because we are in need of an
idea, but because we are hungry for a Person who
is big enough to take all of our problems, resolve
them in Himself, and give comfort. A little girl
came to her father and said, "Daddy, I'm tired.
Let me sit in your lap." Her father said, "Why
don't you just lie down on the couch for a while?"
To which the little girl replied, "I'm not that kind
of tired. I'm tired for you. If you would hold me,
I'd feel lots better," and she snuggled contentedly
in her father's arms. We have come to the point
in our world fatigue where ideas do not make
adequate couches. We need the feel of those
"everlasting arms," the strong arms of Jesus,
which are longing to enfold us, to reassure us, to
comfort.

He invites us, secondly, to a cross. It is impossible to come to the cross and leave it the same
person. Wasn't it Pilgrim in *Pilgrim's Progress*
who saw a vision of a large number of people
struggling up a steep hill with burdens on their
backs, and then saw them coming down the other
side of that hill with their burdens gone? And
didn't he see on the top of that hill a cross, and
at the bottom of that cross a huge pile of burdens?
And didn't he notice that though the pile grew
and grew, the cross, too, grew and grew? It is always more than adequate.

We are told that in certain parts of the world

the roads for miles and miles are thronged with religious pilgrims who are walking, or crawling, to worship at their shrines. As they walk and crawl, they carry large sacks filled with their offerings. They hope to give these offerings as a purchase price for their peace. But they always leave that shrine with their burdens merely transferred from their backs to their hearts, and return home for another year of dreary preparation for the same heart-rending ritual.

Is that what coming to the cross of Jesus means for us this Lenten season? "No," you say. Then why is there so little genuine demonstration of Christian joy among us? For all too many Christians, the peace of God is still a hope, something which may come tomorrow, but somehow has not come yet. We go through with our pilgrimages Sunday after Sunday, communion service after communion service, Lent after Lent, and find a momentary respite, but no deep, abiding peace. And Jesus meant that we find in Him that calm assurance which is so much our need.

It is the ever-present pitfall of works-righteousness which snares us. Not that we believe anything so crass as that we shall enter heaven on the strength of all our good deeds. We have learned quite well that we are saved by faith and not by works. But we manage a subtle shift of emphasis, so that our religious expressions in themselves become our good deeds. Our Bible reading, our worship, yes, our attendance at communion can so easily become a bribe, in exchange for which God will give us His peace. It is only when we see that everything we do, including our worship, is merely a response, a doxology because of what we have already received, that we have peace.

For Jesus is our peace. He has made our peace. We must get out of our own way, and permit peace to enter into our hearts. Only then can assurance visit us. Only then can we know we are His. Then we, too, will say with the colored girl who found Christ at a youth camp, "Now I'se got a light in my heart."

Isaiah tells us about Jesus, "He is a man of sorrows and acquainted with grief. . . . Surely He hath borne our griefs, and carried our sorrows. The chastisement of our *peace* was upon Him." He has bought our peace. He took that weary pilgrimage for us. He endured that defeat for us. And remember—He didn't do this for the good people, for the religious people, for the Bible student, the minister, or the Board of Deacons. He did it for the bad people, the rebellious people, the tired people.

If this is true—and the Bible record never contradicts it—there is only one thing for us to do. We must come. Come, then, will you? Come *with* your problems, *with* your nervousness, *with* your burdens, *with* your sorrows, *with* your worries, *with* your fears. Enter His presence with a prayer, and tell Him that life is too much for you, that you need help and need it badly. Come *with* your temptations. They are really nothing to be ashamed of. Tell Him frankly of the tug and pull within yourself. Come *with* your sins. The shadow of the past has nullified the effectiveness of countless lives. Unforgiven sin, undefeated sin is ruining millions daily. Tell Him that you are undeserving. Tell Him you resent Him, if you do. Keep nothing from Him. But above all, come! Come as you are. Don't wait to improve. Come!

One final word. We as Christians and a Christian Church are supposed to provide the same rallying point for our generation and for other people that Jesus has provided for us. We are supposed to be the voice of Jesus for others. We are supposed to be able to overlook men's sins and see their needs, to forget their religious differences and remember their wants. Do we do this? A minister was taking a course in counseling in a large university. He met an interesting young man who was in the same class. The young man asked him about his life work, and upon hearing that he was a pastor, remarked in honest amazement, "I didn't know that ministers or the Church were concerned with people's problems." And he meant it!

This misunderstanding is growing apace. We stand in danger of letting an imitation, namely psychiatry, take over our rightful role as the help of the helpless. Is this because we have been too hasty in our application of the law, too quick to judge? Is it because we have forgotten how we ourselves were found by God in Jesus? God found us dirty, troubled, tired. Do you remember? The bishop, who said as he approached a drunkard, "There, but for the grace of God, go I," preserved the spirit in which the Christian must always meet his fellow men. We must never lose this spirit, or we shall be made completely ineffective in our dealings with others.

God help us to be the voice of Jesus, for our own world! To be this voice we must quit arguing and start loving. We must be willing to be foolish for our faith. Yes, we must be willing to be stepped upon, taken advantage of, ridiculed as being too "soft." We must demonstrate this peace with which God has blessed us. "The peace which passeth understanding" is more than a benediction at the end of a service. It is not absence of problems, but presence of power, God's power. God help us to be the oil on troubled waters, the deep calm in the center of the world's storm, the "messengers of peace"!

"Come, ye disconsolate, where'er ye languish,
  Come to the mercy-seat, fervently kneel;
  Here bring your wounded hearts, here tell your
    anguish;
  Earth has no sorrow that Heaven cannot heal."